INTELLIGENCE IN ACTION

INTELLIGENCE

BRYANT J. CRATTY

University of California, Los Angeles

IN ACTION

physical activities
for
enhancing intellectual abilities

PRENTICE-HALL, INC., Englewood Cliffs, New Jersey

Library of Congress Cataloging in Publication Data

CRATTY, BRYANT J
  Intelligence in action.

  Includes bibliographies.
    1. Perceptual-motor learning. 2. Educational
games. I. Title. [DNLM: 1. Intelligence.
2. Learning. 3. Physical education and training.
4. Problem solving. WS 105 C8961i 1973]
LB1067.C68   372.1'3   72-7380
ISBN 0-13-469049-4

INTELLIGENCE IN ACTION
Bryant J. Cratty
© 1973 by
PRENTICE-HALL, INC.
Englewood Cliffs, New Jersey

10 9 8 7 6 5 4 3 2 1

Printed in the United States of America

PRENTICE-HALL INTERNATIONAL, INC., *London*
PRENTICE-HALL OF AUSTRALIA, PTY. LTD., *Sydney*
PRENTICE-HALL OF CANADA, LTD., *Toronto*
PRENTICE-HALL OF INDIA PRIVATE LIMITED, *New Delhi*
PRENTICE-HALL OF JAPAN, INC., *Tokyo*

*This book is dedicated to children who try to think
and to the teachers who try to let them try.*

preface

Since the end of World War II, there has been a marked interest in this country, in Europe, and in other parts of the world, in the placement of physical activities within the total educational program for both normal and atypical children. Much of this interest has lead to speculations that various kinds of movement experiences will exert a positive change upon various social, emotional, perceptual, and intellectual abilities.

Writers attempting to delineate movement methodologies, however, have not always precisely matched objectives with program content. At times, speculations out of tune with contemporary knowledge about transfer of training have been advanced, which suggest that engaging in rather simple motor acts will enhance complex intellectual and/or perceptual processes. In this book I have attempted to reverse the trend, and to provide an alternative to this type of speculation. The purpose of this volume is to illustrate just how one may, with relative precision, match program content with objectives that include intellectual improvement. Moreover, the book contains ways in which movement experiences may be employed to tax the intellectual abilities of children.

Upon writing this book, it quickly became apparent that one may truly inculcate virtually any intellectual ability into a lesson in which movement experiences are a main ingredient. While it is of course not necessary to use action to enhance thought, motor activities are both motivating as well as easily observable by teachers, and thus not only encourage children to participate, but also provide the observing instructor with vivid "feedback" of the quality of intellectual effort which has been engaged in by their youthful charges.

The contents of this book are meant to be suggestive rather than prescriptive. The ideas contained in these pages may be expanded upon almost without end. For example, if one is interested in generating political thinking in the minds of elementary school age children, games may provide stimulating springboards for discussion of such concepts as power, coalitions, conflict, and similar concepts. The games involving coding and decoding that are described in the book may be similarly employed in a large variety of ways. Some teachers reviewing this material and my previous work (*Active Learning,* Prentice-Hall) have devised ingenious modifications of equipment. For example, the often cumbersome letter and number grids may be projected on a vertical surface using a slide projector, permitting children to throw and to run and to point to their responses to questions and problems posed. Numerous others have adapted this type of approach to learning to various kinds of atypical children, including the partially sighted, the deaf, the motor handicapped, and the emotionally disturbed. Still others are finding this type of learning method, employing movement, as highly useful for the pre-school age normal child and the normal child in the early primary grades.

Many people have helped me discover some of the ideas contained in this text. Some of these are colleagues from other countries while others are American psychologists, notably John Guilford, Jerome Bruner, and others whose work has provided helpful guidelines. The influence of Jean Piaget is also obvious in what follows.

My office staff, notably Donna Hokoda and Brian Tash, have aided me with the typing and editing of this manuscript, as they have on numerous other occasions in the past. I am particularly grateful to Retta Scott Worcester who so wonderfully created the illustrations for this text and for *Active Learning*. I believe that her work has materially aided the presentation of these ideas. I am also indebted to Walter Welch and the editors of Prentice-Hall, for the faith they have had in my work during the past several years. Most of all, I would like to thank the children whom I have worked with in numerous demonstrations in many states of the Union, as well as within schools of special education and regular education in the Los Angeles area. It was while observing and questioning them that most of the following ideas began to unfold.

B.C.J.

contents

three : CATEGORIZATION   43

four : LANGUAGE COMMUNICATION   67

INTELLIGENCE
IN ACTION

one

INTRODUCTION

Available records indicate that from the dawn of written history, man has evidenced concern about the nature of intelligence. Philosophical writings dating back to the Golden Age of Greece, and even before, point to the interest in how learning takes place, in what ways memory may be enhanced, and how events are organized and interpreted.

These same concerns may be traced throughout writings by scholars in more recent history. Two parallel and related problems have emerged: (a) What is the makeup of human intellectual endeavors? and (b) How may cognitive functioning be enhanced through exposure to formal and informal educational experiences?

The beginnings of the intellectual awakening occurred during the late 1700's and early 1800's, when these problems began to be explored in the rational, orderly ways dictated by the newly discovered scientific methods of problem solving. For example, during the early nineteenth century, physicians began to assess and evaluate the abilities—physical and mental—of retarded children so that they might be assigned to homes for the retarded; while some teachers in Europe were formulating systematic ways for improving the communicative efforts of the deaf and the intellectual behaviors of the less gifted children in their midst.

Careful scrutiny of the literature during the centuries also discloses that various attempts have been made to pair physical activity with intellectual endeavor. In antiquity, the Greek mind-body idealism was manifested in art as well as in literature; Greek statues were marked by intelligent, keen-eyed faces atop well-muscled torsos. Plato has been quoted as saying: "In teaching young children, train them by a kind of game, and you will be able to see more clearly the natural bent of each."

The humanists of later centuries also incorporated movement activities within the educational programs they espoused. They hoped in this way to preserve the natural inclinations of the child to move and to explore while confronting him with academic content. The French writer Fénelon, who died in 1715, observed that some children could learn to read while playing. The close association between the child's mind and body espoused by Rousseau, Froebel, and others in later years is well known to students of educational philosophy.

Relationships between intellectual and physical functions were also explored by the first experimental psychologists in England, the United States, and Germany toward the latter part of the 1800's. Since some of the first psychological experiments by Wilhelm Wundt in Leipzig involved tests of simple sensory-motor functioning, and tests of reaction time, visual following, and the accuracy of the "muscle sense," it seemed logical to some of his colleagues, as well as to J. McKeen Cattell in America and Sir Francis Galton in England, to determine whether these basic measures were in some way predictive of so-called higher intellectual functions. They were aided in their search by Karl Pearson, a young student of Galton's, and others who began to develop and refine basic statistical tools, including the concepts underlying averaging, distribution statistics and correlation coefficients. Observing the obvious motor incoordination in many retarded children, these early experimental psychologists sought to determine whether basic motor and sensory measures could predict the degree of academic and cognitive abilities possessed by individuals at several points along the scale of intelligence.

However, careful comparisons of the manner in which basic tests of sensory and motor functioning ranked people, from the most to the least proficient, contrasted to the way in which tests of verbal comprehension, problem-solving abilities, and similar measures ranked these same individuals, failed to disclose even moderate relationships. Thus, despite the obvious fact that the severely retarded inevitably evidence rather marked motor problems, children with subnormal, average, or superior intelligence were found to reflect a wide variety of basic movement attributes when exposed to simple laboratory tests sampling the quality of their sensory and motor faculties.

Towards the turn of this century, Alfred Binet, introducing the concept of mental levels, began to demonstrate that if one wished to discriminate between the intellectual functioning of children of various ages or between those assigned to schools for the retarded and those within the usual educational confines, batteries containing tests that sampled vocabulary, verbal comprehension, problem-solving abilities, and quantitative operations were the only useful tools.

During these same years, however, several educators persisted in the belief that placing the child in action might have educational advantages, and that certain performance tests might be at least partly predictive of how a child might function in life situations. Thus, for example, standardized I.Q. tests began to be expanded to include "performance" items, which were intended to tap certain perceptual and motor qualities. Stanley Porteus, an Australian, painstakingly constructed a written maze test which he felt was not only applicable in primative cultures as a test of coping, but also was helpful in determining the practical abilities of retarded children and the extent to which they might fit into vocational training situations.

Educational strategies incorporating basic sensory and motor experiences, sometimes paired and sometimes engaged in separately, were also explored by such pioneers as Itard and his young student, Sequin, working with the retarded in France; while an even more codified system of education for the culturally deprived child employing movement experiences was developed by Maria Montessori in Rome during the first part of the twentieth century.

The majority of Montessori's activities involved manual manipulation of materials and attending to concepts made concrete through exposure to various senses. Several of the strategies she employed involved the use of the total body in actions requiring involvement of the larger muscle groups. For example, she believed that developing the balance abilities of young children was important, and within some of the "purer" Montessori programs today, one may see two- and three-year-olds walking around lines to music, while carefully holding long-stemmed champagne glasses filled with water.

Dr. Montessori also advocated games containing academic content for the young normal child, and the atypical child. For example, the "Egg Crate" game was a popular one in some of the early Montessori schools. In this game, twelve children stood in the center of the room "like a dozen eggs" and then were asked to divide in half, count themselves, and then say, "How many are there in half a dozen?" The game was continued by having the children divide into smaller equal-size groups and assess the number of children in the divisions that resulted.

Although the incidence of these happy kinds of academic experiences seemed to diminish in schools during the early decades of the twentieth century, writings by Strauss and Lehtinen shortly after World War II brought forth another burst of interest in the motor component of the human personality. These observant clinicians highlighted the fact that there are a considerable number of children competing within regular school classrooms who are less than adequate perceptually, are often hyperactive, and in many cases evidence motor coordination problems. Moreover, these clinicians advocated remedial methods, intended to improve the general academic competence of children they described as "brain injured."

During the years immediately following, some educators focused considerable attention upon the movement part of the "Strauss syndrome," and began to advocate a number of programs of motor activities which purportedly had effects upon a child's total educational efforts.

From the late 1950's until the present time, descriptions of these various movement programs have been the subject of a great many books and journals, and have attracted the attention of large numbers of parents and educators both in the United States and abroad.

In general these more recent theories relating movement to intellectual endeavor may be classified according to the nature of their theoretical underpinnings within the following four categories.[1] Some have advocated what might be termed a *perceptual-motor approach* to expanding human abilities through exposure to movement activities. Such writers as Getman and Newell Kephart, noting the manner in which infants seem to explore their worlds in direct ways, have suggested that motor activities are imperatives for the development of perceptual abilities, and the latter are the basic supports of all learning, including academic tasks requiring higher levels of intellectual functioning. Thus, as would be expected, their programs advocate the extensive use of movement activities, sometimes paired with visual exploration, which will purportedly heighten the child's perceptual awareness of his world and lead to more successful functioning in a variety of endeavors.

Others, notably the Doman-Delacato group in Philadelphia, have put forth a model which reminds one of the recapitulation theories of sixteenth- and seventeenth-century philosophers. Essentially they maintain that the child passes through stages of development that parallel in marked ways those through which the human being evolved from his earliest beginnings as a water animal. Reflex writhings seen in human infants, these writers contend, are similar to the wigglings of fish, and later attempts at locomotion and manipulative acts seen in the developing child are similar to efforts evidenced by amphibians, mammals, and primates. As a result of this kind of speculation, the motor program they advocate contains several basic movement activities resembling the attempts of animals to move through space, such as creeping, crawling, and the like.[2] The Doman-Delacato group suggest that, through exposure to these and similar activities, some kind of adjustment in the *neurological organization* of a child may take place, and a variety of abilities and disabilities reflecting intellectual and perceptual functioning may be affected in positive ways.

Others have advocated what might be termed a *dynamic approach* to explain how engaging in motor activities may positively

---

[1] Inspection of the practices advocated by the various theoreticians reveals a remarkable similarity, with only a few exceptions.

[2] More thorough accounts of these methods, and the research supporting and failing to support them, are contained in Myers and Hammill, *Methods for Learning Disorders* (New York: John Wiley & Sons, Inc., 1969), and in Cratty, *Perceptual and Motor Development in Infants and Children* (New York: The Macmillan Company, 1970).

change other facets of the growing child's personality. Research by James Oliver in England and Ernest Kiphard in Germany have produced data suggesting that an improvement in the self-concept of a child through pleasurable and successful experiences in physical activity may also result in increased effort toward tasks reflecting intellectual as well as motor functioning. Thus, it is hypothesized that between engaging in movement tasks and later observed intellectual improvement, there is an important intermediate factor, the ego, or "self," which if strengthened will be reflected in a more integrated and stable personality, one better able to cope with tasks in the classroom as well as on the ball field. Those who concentrate upon improving children afflicted with motor clumsiness have strongly suggested that this "dynamic theory" is a viable one upon which to rest their efforts.

A fourth approach attempts to improve intellectual performance through participation in movement activities based upon what might be termed *cognitive models*. In general, this theory suggests that to enhance intellectual functions and academic operations through movement experiences, one must pair, in precise ways, the movement activities with the intellectual qualities one hopes to change. Mindlessly applied and mindlessly accepted motor tasks are not likely to change anything but motor function, it is explained. Instead, those who put forth this theory believe that one must in specific manners incorporate in movement programs the various types of perceptual, cognitive, and academic tasks one hopes to change. Among the proponents of this general model are Jean Le Boulch, Louis Picq, and Pierre Vayer in France; and James Humphrey and Muska Mosston in the United States. This fourth approach is the one undergirding the material contained in this text.

Why Does Movement Work?

Movement activities may affect children's proficiency in tasks which require thought and perceptual abilities for several reasons.

1. Motor activities usually require the close attention and concern of some interested adult figure. Frequently this "attention effect" alone is sufficient to encourage a child to perform better in a variety of tasks to which he is later exposed. Some of the "success stories" which have emanated from the Doman-Delacato program may be attributed to the fact that the family is given some kind of purportedly helpful way to work with one of their members;

and the child when given this extra and prolonged attention may blossom.

Experimenters, when designing research studies intended to explore the effects of an activity program, must, in order for their findings to be considered valid, include a group of subjects to which only special attention is accorded, in order to separate these effects from factors intrinsic to the program under consideration.

2. Programs of motor training may keep children away from onerous classroom activities in which they may be failing to achieve; the resultant spacing of practice in the former enables some of their inhibitions to the task to dissipate. Research dating back more than sixty years has indicated, for example, that spacing practice of verbal skills has a beneficial effect upon performance levels achieved. Thus, helpful spacing of reading is sometimes the result of replacing practice in reading with motor training two or more times a week.

It is obvious that the two reasons outlined above are what might be termed indirect benefits, and could occur within any kind of special kind of enrichment program, whether or not motor activity was an intrinsic part. More specifically, the following factors have been observed (and measured) to aid academic improvement when children are exposed to movement experiences in which academic content is an integral part.

1. The games are fun. Motivating practice of what might have been oppressive academic skills produces better learning when contrasted to academic enrichment programs in which the children are kept within passive conditions.

2. An active approach to learning academic skills many times provides a natural "match" between program content and the needs some children have to be active.

Studies of babies at birth reflect vast inherent differences in activity levels. These same activity level differences are seen in preschool children, and are even reflected in behaviors, job choices, and similar measures later in life. One researcher has found that people may be divided into two categories—the "reducers," those with high activity needs, with an accompanying tendency to be less perceptive, and the "augmenters," who tend to be sensitive to pain, and to kinesthetic as well as visual stimulation. The latter might be expected to do well within passive classroom settings, while the former might not be expected to do so. Finally, studies in Scandinavia have shown that confining the more physically fit children to prolonged periods of classroom study and testing may make them less capable of performing academically by the end of the school day, as contrasted to children who are less fit, and who may possess lower needs for activity.

3. When the total body is in action, participating in a game in which academic or intellectual abilities are being taxed, it is difficult for the child to attend to extraneous conditions or stimuli. Hopping in squares containing letters, counting aloud while doing so, and looking at the letters at the same time permit the child to become preoccupied with little else. There are numerous research studies attesting to the importance of quality of attention to tasks, as contrasted merely to practice trials, in the enhancement of learning and performance improvement. Physical activities in which the child must be totally engrossed may tend to produce that type of qualitative attention to the task.

4. Studies of some children within the central parts of some of our larger cities indicate that while their values include a high regard for physical activity and verbal abilities, there is likely to be a less high regard for some phases of academic learning, including reading. Indeed, in one study it was found that some ghetto youths did not know, nor care, whether their best friends could read or not. Using active games as a learning methodology tends to pair a pleasurable and highly regarded activity with one that may not be as highly valued, and thus might give more pleasure to the practice of the academic skill.

5. Further studies of the cognitive strategies employed by some "central-city" children and youth indicate that they are often more comfortable dealing with concrete situations, rather than those in the abstract. Movement activities provide concrete acts to experience, to observe, and to think about. Furthermore, these kinds of concrete and obvious response patterns can be incorporated well into philosophies of education, in which what are termed "measurable behavioral objectives" play an important part.

6. Movement activities with the reflection of thought, and when paired with academic tasks of various kinds, provide the teacher with observable evidence of the *quality* of a child's thought processes. Subtle intellectual machinations occurring while seated at a desk are not as easily seen, identified, modified, or evaluated by an instructor.

In summary, it appears that there are many pervasive reasons why a more active approach might enhance children's learning. In essence, however, it is not advanced that *all* children need to be placed in action to truly learn best. There is a mountain of evidence that, indeed, silent and relatively immobile contemplation is desirable at times, in many circumstances, and on the part of many children, youth, and adults. Rather, the previous evidence has been advanced to indicate how *some* children may benefit if a more expansive look is taken not only at the direction and content of curricula, but also at how intensely the curricula may be presented.

What Follows

Previous texts by James Humphrey, by this writer, and by others have presented in very operational terms how specific kinds of games might enhance the acquisition of reading and prereading competencies, spelling and mathematical operations, language functions, and science concepts. Relatively little is available that illustrates how more basic *intellectual strategies* may be operationalized in the form of active tasks in which the larger muscles of the body are involved.

The exception to this is the text by Mosston (1966), but here again various kinds of problem-solving behaviors researched by Guilford (1968), Gagné (1965), and others are not treated in detail. Instead, Mosston simply suggests that cognitive development is mainly the product of shifting decisions about the educational processes from instructor to student.

The chapters that follow will take a deeper and broader approach to the exposition of just how vigorous motor activities may both reflect and stimulate certain intellectual abilities and operations. Although no attempt has been made to explore in detail the various cognitive models which have been developed within the past thirty years by Piaget, Guilford, Gagné, and others, their type of research has strongly influenced the content of this book.[3]

The intent of this text is to expose teachers to practical axamples of how a child's intellectual abilities may be stimulated through various kinds of movement problems, as well as via traditional childhood games seen on the playground. Despite the fact that children in modern societies have been noted to engage in games requiring high-level thought to an increasing degree within recent years, their bodies retain the need for movement experiences in order to function well. It is hoped that the examples of activities outlined on the following pages may be expanded upon by creative teachers,

---

[3] A more thorough exploration may be found in Cratty, *Physical Expressions of Intelligence* (Englewood Cliffs, N. J.: Prentice-Hall, Inc., 1972).

while at the same time the ideas advanced may prove amenable to verification or rejection by researchers who may be "caught up" within this potentially useful and fascinating way to stimulate and educate children and youth.

The material which follows has been divided into several sections, roughly corresponding to often-seen categories of intellectual functioning. Chapter 2 contains activities to enhance, or at least stimulate, selected memory abilities. Thus, tasks involving short-term as well as long-term memory, for visual as well as auditory information, are outlined.

Chapter 3 contains work involving the child's ability to categorize. Activities in which movements may be placed into categories, as well as active games in which the child may be encouraged to categorize both visual and auditory information, are presented. This ability to form categories of ever-increasing precision, according to many observers, is one of the primary ways in which an adequate intelligence is manifested.

Chapter 4 is devoted to activities that couple well with practice in language communication—development of speech, reading, comprehension.

Chapter 5 presents movement games that involve evaluative processes. In some the child is asked to evaluate himself, in others he must determine the qualitative or quantitative efforts of others; still others deal with his ability to ascertain individual differences among groups of children, or in groups in which he may be a part.

Chapter 6 contains activities which reflect various kinds of problem-solving behavior. Tasks reflecting both convergent, as well as divergent, thinking are found in this section, together with tasks which require the abilities to analyze and to synthesize complex situations. Other situations which require that the child perceive the manner in which the processes or constituent parts may be reversed are also outlined in this section.

Chapter 7 analyzes the intellectual components of a popular children's game. The final chapter is an overview, with guidelines for incorporating this type of program and games into the total school curriculum.

Reviewing the material, it is immediately apparent that there are relatively few tasks involving a "pure" type of intellectual behavior. For the most part, every task requires various processes working together, or in sequence, in order to find an adequate solution. Because several scholars studying cognition and intellectual behavior employ the same terms for different processes or different terms for the same processes, this book is careful to sort out and organize for the reader just what abilities are purportedly contributing to task performance.

To assist in this sorting-out process, the games are presented in the following manner, after a brief chapter introduction reviewing the nature of the general ability under consideration.

First, the objective is stated—What qualities and intellectual processes is the activity intended to enhance? Second, the requirements are listed—number and ages of participants, equipment needed, and the like. Third, a description of the game is given, containing the "script" which the teacher may generally follow, the expected responses from the children (both verbal and motor), and the appropriate teacher responses thereto. Finally, suggestions are made for modifying the activity to meet children's needs for greater complexity, or to offer more variety with continued exposure.

This text is not intended to provide an educational cure-all for children who are bright, average, or underachievers. Rather, it is hoped that the overall direction and suggestions presented will encourage further experimentation on the part of sensitive, innovative instructors. Exploration along these lines, if applied with enthusiasm and understanding, cannot fail to reward the participants in such a program. Youngsters have everything to gain from engaging in activities that are both physically and mentally invigorating.

BIBLIOGRAPHY

BLOOM, BENJAMIN S., ed. *Taxonomy of Educational Objectives, Handbook I: Cognitive Domain.* New York: David McKay Co., Inc., 1956.

BRUNER, JEROME S. "The Course of Cognitive Growth," in *American Psychologist* 19 (January 1964): 1–15.

CATTELL, J. MCKEEN. "Mental Tests and Measurements," in *Mind* 15 (1890): 373–80.

CHANEY, CLARA, and KEPHART, NEWELL C. *Motoric Aids to Perceptual Training.* Columbus, Ohio: Charles E. Merrill Books, Inc., 1968.

CRATTY, BRYANT J. *Active Learning.* Englewood Cliffs, N.J.: Prentice-Hall, Inc., 1971.

————. "Evaluation and Discussion of Selected Perceptual-Motor

Programs Purporting to Enhance Academic Function," in *Perceptual and Motor Development in Infants and Children.* New York: The Macmillan Company, 1970.

————. *Human Behavior and Learning: Understanding Educational Processes.* Wolfe City, Texas: University Press, 1972.

————. *Physical Expressions of Intelligence.* Englewood Cliffs, N.J.: Prentice-Hall, Inc., 1972.

————, and MARTIN, SISTER MARGARET MARY. *The Effects of a Program of Learning Games Upon Selected Academic Abilities of Children with Learning Difficulties.* Washington, D.C.: U.S. Office of Education, Bureau of Education for the Handicapped, 1970.

————, and SZCZEPANIK, SISTER MARK. *The Effects of a Program of Learning Games Upon Selected Academic Abilities in Retarded Children with Low Academic Potential.* Washington, D.C.: U.S. Office of Education, Bureau of Education for the Handicapped, 1971.

DELACATO, CARL H. *The Diagnosis and Treatment of Speech and Reading Problems.* Springfield, Ill.: Charles C. Thomas, Publisher, 1963.

GAGNÉ, R. W. "The Analysis of Instructional Objectives for the Design of Instruction," in Robert Glaser, ed. *Teaching Machines and Programmed Learning, II: Data and Directions.* Department of Audiovisual Instruction, National Education Association, Washington, D.C., 1965.

————. *The Conditions of Learning.* New York: Holt, Rinehart & Winston, Inc., 1965.

GALTON, SIR FRANCIS. *Inquiries Into Human Faculty and Its Development.* London: E.P. Dutton & Co., 1883.

GODFREY, BARBARA B., and KEPHART, NEWELL C. *Movement Patterns and Motor Education.* New York: Appleton-Century-Crofts, 1969.

GUILFORD, J. P. *Intelligence, Creativity, and their Educational Implications.* San Diego, Calif.: Robert R. Knapp, Publisher, 1968.

————. *The Nature of Human Intelligence.* New York: McGraw-Hill Book Company, 1967.

————. "Three Faces of Intellect," in *American Psychologist* 14 (1959): 469–79.

HUMPHREY, JAMES, and SULLIVAN, DOROTHY. *Teaching Slow Learners Through Active Games.* Springfield, Ill.: Charles C. Thomas, Publisher, 1970.

ITARD, JEAN-MARC GASPARD. *The Wild Boy of Aveyron,* translated by George and Muriel Humphrey. New York: Appleton-Century-Crofts, 1932.

LE BOULCH, JEAN. *L'Education par le mouvement* (Education Through Movement). Paris: Les Editions Sociales Françaises, 1967.

MOSSTON, MUSKA. *Teaching Physical Education.* Columbus, Ohio: Charles E. Merrill Books, Inc., 1966.

MYERS, PATRICIA I., and HAMMILL, DONALD D. *Methods for Learning Disorders.* New York: John Wiley & Sons, Inc., 1969.

PIAGET, JEAN. *The Early Growth of Logic in the Child,* translated by E. A. Lunzer and D. Papert. London: Routledge & Kegan Paul, Ltd., 1964.

————. *The Language and Thought of the Child,* translated by M. Gabain. London: Routledge & Kegan Paul, Ltd., 1926.

————. *The Origins of Intelligence in Children,* translated by M. Cook. New York: International University Press, 1952.

PICQ, LOUIS, and VAYER, PIERRE. *Education Psycho-Motrice.* Paris: Editions Doin-Derem et Cie, 1968.

POPHAM, W. JAMES, and BAKER, EVA L. *Systematic Instruction.* Englewood Cliffs, N.J.: Prentice-Hall, Inc., 1970.

PORTEUS, STANLEY D. *The Maze Test and Clinical Psychology.* Palo Alto, Calif.: Pacific Books, 1959.

SEGUIN, EDWARD. *Idiocy: Its Treatment by the Physiological Method.* New York: Bureau of Publications, Teachers College, Columbia University, 1907.

STRAUSS, A. A., and LEHTINEN, L. E. *Psychopathology and Education of the Brain-Injured Child.* New York: Grune & Stratton, Inc., 1947.

WISEMAN, STEPHEN, ed. *Intelligence and Ability.* Baltimore: Penguin Books, Inc., 1967.

two

MEMORIZATION

Memorization has been listed by most scholars as one of the more basic intellectual operations. Speculation about the many ramifications of human memory has an interesting historical background. The ancient Greeks practiced various types of memory aids which are found in contemporary programs of self-improvement. Greek orators, for example, often paired various parts of their speech with spatial reference points (such as rooms in the temple), and as they gave their speech they would "mentally travel" from room to room, upon whose walls they had imagined their words were written.

There are many facets of the study of memory which have caught the interest of researchers. The order in which serially presented material is learned, for example, has been a commonly researched learning phenomenon; during more recent times, the tendency of an individual to "chunk" or group large amounts of material so that it may be more easily acquired has been the topic of several research efforts.

Memory has also been studied within several time dimensions. For example, human factors researchers and others who have been struck with the similarities between the human mind and computers have suggested that information to be remembered may be "dropped" into the individual's long-term, short-term, or medium-term memory storage bin. A second temporal dimension to the study of memory involves the processes important in mental rehearsal and how one may translate material presented into forms which result in its retention over a reasonably long interval.

Several programs of movement education, as well as several tests which purport to evaluate the child's body image and body concept, require imitation of the movements or gestures of an instructor or of another child. Examples of some of these activities are some of the games that follow.

Short-Term Serial Memory and Imitation

A number of programs, including one I have researched, contain tasks which purportedly enhance short-term memory via the imitation of various movements presented in sequence. These tasks may require a child to react in one or more of several ways.

1. Repeating, while blindfolded, in correct sequence a number of gestures, beginning with two, after first visually inspecting the movements.

2. Reproducing two or more gestures in correct order without a blindfold, after first visually inspecting the gestures.

3. Reproducing a series of body positions originally presented via flash cards.

4. Remembering and repeating a series of movements through a maze constructed of boxes or similar objects.

5. Remembering and repeating, in the same order, a series of bodily movements made within geometric configurations on the ground. (Reproduction may be done via verbal directions or by first visually inspecting the series of movements and then repeating them.)

6. Remembering and reproducing a series of locations to which a child has previously "traveled."

Other dimensions which have been suggested for this kind of short-term serial memory task involve delays between the time a series of movements are performed and the time when the inspecting child must imitate them.

Critical to the evaluation of these programs, which have been advanced purportedly to enhance serial memory ability, are two related questions: (a) How general or specific is serial memory? (b) Can practice in tasks involving serial memory of movements enhance the child's ability to remember a series of other kinds of stimuli (words, letters, information received auditorily, etc.)?

From the results of a pilot study of children in grades 1 to 4, it was found that there was a moderate to high positive correlation between serial memory tasks, indicating that to some degree serial memory ability taps some general memory quality in the young children tested. It is possible that serial memory tasks executed by older children and by adults, involving different input modes, would not evidence the same high positive relationship.

In an attempt to answer the second question, the same subjects in this study were given tests to determine how well they would retain a series of numbers given verbally and how well they could recite in correct order a series of pictures which were presented visually. After being exposed to serial memory games involving movement imitation, the experimental group evidenced improvement in serial memory tasks involving the ordering of words in a series, remembering the order of numbers presented auditorily, and the replication of the order of animal pictures presented visually. Although additional research on this topic is needed, the results of this study were highly encouraging.

Tasks emphasizing the serial memory of movements are potentially helpful to educators and to the participating children because the quality of the child's memory ability is immediately apparent to all concerned. Moreover, data from other sources suggest that measures of serial memory are correlated both to measures of attention and to scores reflecting what is termed "perceptual span" (the ability to remember the nature of a group of stimuli quickly presented via a tachistoscope).

Our observations of children engaged in this type of serial memory task involving movements suggest that their attention is good and that the games are highly motivating. The children in our program often request additional games of this nature at the completion of a lesson; their additional participation forms a reward for their previous efforts on other tasks.

Long-Term Memory, Semantics, and Symbols

Other movement experiences which will purportedly heighten a child's ability to remember, over an extended time period, the shapes of letters, geometric figures, words, and similar symbolic and semantic content are found in my book, *Active Learning.*

These games have been applied in various ways and to children of all ages and varying degrees of intellectual capacity. Moreover, creative teachers have elaborated upon their content, aiding in the translation of the sound of words from viewing their shapes, and vice versa.

GAME 1   Can You Do It Too?

To Enhance: Short-term serial memory of visual stimuli.

Participants: From two to twenty children, ages 5 to 10.

Description: One child performs a gesture using the upper limbs, with the body fixed, e.g., holds the right arm up in the air. The other children attempt to repeat gesture.

Performing child then adds a second gesture to the first, e.g., places left hand on hip. Again the observing children attempt to repeat.

Teacher should now say, "We will keep adding more gestures of this nature until you start to have difficulty remembering each one."

Questions to Children: How can you remember three or more gestures in sequence? Expected answers: "By repeating them to ourselves with words," or perhaps "By imagining ourselves doing them," or maybe "By imagining another child doing them." This could lead into a discussion of how each of us learns and remembers differently, and of how various kinds of imagery may enhance short-term memory and "deposit" short-term material into the "long-term memory storage."

Other questions teacher might ask: "Is all information we receive worth remembering?" "How can we decide what to remember, and for how long?"

Modifications: After imitating three or more movements, have the children perform them with eyes closed.

Gestures may be added in sequences, until six, seven or eight are reached.

Limb gestures may be alternated with movements of the total body.

Static positions may be alternated with movements of the limbs or the total body.

For further practice in the ability to mentally rehearse movements or positions in a series, have the children pause 10, 20, 30, or 60 seconds before attempting to imitate the movements demonstrated.

GAME 2 Where Did He (or She) Go?

To Enhance: Short-term serial memory of visual or auditory stimuli.

Participants and Equipment: From two to twenty children, mental age 4 or 5. Configurations taped to the floor, as shown, or painted on asphalt or cement.

Description: A demonstrator is asked to go to one or more configurations, returning to a starting point between a "visit" to each.

Observers must then remember the order in which each configuration was visited, and demonstrate this retention by visiting them in the same order.

Increasing difficulty may be introduced by an increased number of visits to be remembered. Children take turns being observer and demonstrator.

Modifications: Child with eyes closed may be *told* by an observing child what configurations demonstrator visited.

Demonstrating child may revisit same configuration, but go there in a variety of ways, e.g., skipping, hopping, running, walking.

Observer must then get there in the same ways, performed in the same order.

Three-dimensional objects such as tires, boxes, etc. may be substituted for some or all of the configurations shown.

GAME 3   Remembering Movements

To Enhance: Short-term serial memory for visual stimuli, and for the order in which stimuli are seen.

Participants and Equipment: Three or more children, ages 3 and older. Configurations laid out in semicircle as shown, or boxes, tires, tunnels, etc. similarly placed a short distance apart.

Description: One performing child executes a different movement within each configuration in order, starting with two. Observing child then attempts to repeat movements in the same order, on the same configurations.

Two, three, four, and then more movements are executed in series, with attempts made to repeat them in the same order.

Modifications: Performing child may be asked to repeat his own movements in correct order.

Child may be asked to do a "ball thing" within each configuration— bounce it, roll it around, etc.—with observing children then asked to do likewise.

Delays of increasing length may be introduced between the time series is demonstrated and the time the observers are permitted to react.

Observer may attempt to describe verbally what was done, to a third child who was not permitted to observe demonstration.

GAME 4   Where and What?

To Enhance: Short-term visual memory for movements and for spatial locations; ability to auditorily sequence words and match them with actions.

Participants and Equipment: Children ages 3 and older, depending upon intellectual capabilities. Configurations, as shown in Games 2 and 3.

Description: One child performs a movement within two or more configurations, *not in order*. Observing children must perform same movements in same configurations.

Modifications: "Recorder" may, using a blackboard, make a record of movements and/or location to facilitate memory problem.

Performer may do a "ball thing," or a "left or right" movement in each of the configurations.

Observing child may inform a third child (who has not been permitted to observe demonstration) what the demonstrating child did, and where.

GAME 5   Jumping Ways

To Enhance: Short-term visual memory for movements in series.

Participants and Equipment: Children ages 2, 3, and older. Rope, 10 to 12 feet long.

Description: While two children hold rope still, at an angle, or swing it, demonstrating child must perform two, three, or more movements in series, going over rope as illustrated.

Observing children must repeat series of movements in the correct order.

Modifications: Rope may be placed in irregular position on ground, with series of movements performed along its length and over various of the curves, as shown.

Instead of a rope, a hoop or hoops may be employed to jump into, through, while held vertically, etc.

Again verbal descriptions of movements may be relayed to children who have not had the opportunity to observe initial demonstrations.

Combination course, composed of ropes, hoops, etc., may be employed and children must remember series of movements performed over, under, and between pieces of apparatus.

GAME 6   Around the "Trees"

To Enhance: Short-term serial memory for spatial locations, movements, etc.

Participants and Equipment: Children, or real "trees," black-board.

Description: Three to eight children arrange themselves at various points around the yard, as "trees" with their arms spread out like branches. If real trees are available so much the better.

An "Indian" makes his way through the trees on a pathway which takes him around each "tree."

Observing "trackers" must remember his route, and attempt to duplicate it exactly.

An increasing number of "trees" may be employed for additional difficulty, building up from three or four to seven, eight, or even more.

Modifications: With a blackboard containing the location of the trees, an observer may, following the route traversed by the Indian, attempt to draw a line around the correct trees describing the pathway taken by the Indian.

A tree may be visited by the Indian more than once in his sojourn.

The Indian may lead a child blindfolded around the trees, and then with the blindfold removed, he may try to draw on the blackboard or walk through the pathway he has just taken.

Indians may choose to traverse the route using different means of locomotion from tree to tree (running, skipping, etc.) which also must be duplicated by observers.

GAME 7   Remembering Letters

To Enhance: Long-term memory of letter shapes, letter sounds, and letter characteristics.

Equipment: Mirror, ball, rope, blackboard.

Description: Letter is placed on the board, either lower or upper case. Then observing children, using available equipment (ball, ropes, etc.) and their bodies, attempt to form a similar letter shape.

This may be done in front of a mirror for confirmation. Letter shape may be made through movement through the conformations of the letter, or by static representation of the letter. Crosses for T's and dots for i's may be made with ropes and balls.

Letter must be recognized by observing children, spoken by both demonstrator and observers, and sounded out.

Modifications: "Letters" may be formed in either a horizontal or vertical plane, i.e., while lying down or while standing upright. Letters may be formed by using the trunk, the trunk and limbs, or the limbs and fingers.

Children may attempt, first using a mirror, to make all the letters of the alphabet in order.

Letters may be formed, after first calling out its "sound." More than one letter per sound is of course possible. Letter combinations may also be made in response to various sounds such as *ing, tion,* etc.

For concentrated practice, letters may be broken up into three groups—curved: S, C, O; combination (curved and straight sections): Q, G, B, P, R, etc., and straight lines: K, L, I, T, Y, etc. (Is letter U a curved or a combination letter?)

GAME 8   Remembering Obstacles

To Enhance: Short-term serial memory, visual memory.

Participants and Equipment: Children ages 5 and older; retarded children ages 7 and older. Tires, ropes, balls, boxes, tables, chairs, and other apparatus which would form a three-dimensional obstacle course.

Description: Apparatus placed in a line or semicircle, first child must negotiate two or three obstacles in a given order. Observing

children must remember which obstacles were negotiated, and perform similar movements with each.

Modifications: Movements might be limited to doing something "around" obstacles, or "over," or "into," or "left," or "right," etc. More difficulty can be added by adding obstacles, performing with obstacles out of spatial order, or requiring child who is observing to inform a third child what was accomplished by the first demonstrating child.

Children might discuss differences in the types of movements which were employed to negotiate or otherwise deal with obstacles of various types.

A ball may be employed with some or all obstacles in the course.

GAME 9   Over, Under, Behind, On Top Of

To Enhance: Ability to remember locations, to conceptualize about spatial dimensions of movement and of people in relation to things; acquisition and transfer of spatial concepts.

Participants and Equipment: Three or more children, ages 5 and older. A chair or a small table, a large wooden box, etc.

Description: Using one piece of equipment, a child is asked to do two or more things with his body in relation to the equipment, e.g., go under it, stand on top of it, go around it.

Observing children must then replicate, in the same order, the same things in relation to the equipment employed.

Modifications: An increasing number of things can be done prior to asking for a replication by observers. "Movement things," can be alternated with "ball things." Left things versus right things (i.e., movements) can be executed.

Observing children can write down what they see and read their written observations to children who have not observed the initial demonstration.

Time lapses of increasing duration can be placed between initial demonstration and opportunities for replication by observing children.

Observing child, when he performs, is asked to talk his way through the movements, i.e., explain what he is doing as he does it.

Transfer to "over," "under," "on top of" concepts can be made by requiring observing child to perform the same types of movements, in the same order, but on a different piece of apparatus.

After observing performance, child might be asked to draw spatial concepts on a blackboard instead of performing them himself.

GAME 10   Ball Things

To Enhance: Ball skills, short-term serial memory, visual memory.

Participants and Equipment: Children ages 4, 5, and older. Balls of various sizes.

Description: First child does one or more things with a ball— bounces it a given number of times, throws it in the air to himself, rolls it, etc.

Observing children must then replicate movements in the same order. All children, using their own balls, might perform at once, or each might perform separately.

Modifications: Partner might check on accuracy of replication by performer.

Ball things of increasing difficulty might be performed.

Balls of various sizes and weights might be employed.

Left things versus right things might be performed by initial demonstrators.

Ball things in relation to targets, ropes, boxes, etc. might be initially demonstrated and then replicated.

Time delays might be interpolated between initial demonstration and later replication.

Written descriptions of ball tasks might be carried out, and then read to children who had no opportunity to make direct observations of initial demonstrations.

GAME 11 Animals

To Enhance: Short-term serial memory, analysis of animal behaviors, imagination.

Participants and Equipment: Children ages 3 and older; retarded children ages 5, 6, and older. Ropes, sticks, tumbling mats, blackboard.

Description: First child imitates an animal, e.g., elephant walk with hand for trunk, seal walk dragging legs, rabbit hop, etc. Imitation may or may not be accompanied by appropriate noises. Ropes and sticks may be used as tails, trunks, etc.

Observing children must replicate animal; then second child imitates a second animal, which then must be added to first imitation

by observing children. Animals are then sequentially added, and ever-increasing series must be remembered and imitated sequentially.

Modifications: Blackboard may be used to write down animal names to aid memory, or to draw pictures of animals imitated. Lessons may follow or precede lesson from animal book. Flash cards with animals' names may be employed with children who read.

Teacher may ask for imitations without any animal noises; or may ask for imitations for certain types of animals (those who do work for us, for example).

Children may listen to animal noises and try to imitate animal movements with or without noises.

Demonstrating child may imitate the movements of one animal and the noises of another; observing children may be asked to imitate movements of animals represented by the noises.

GAME 12   Target Throw

To Enhance: Throwing skills, serial memory, visual memory.

Participants and Equipment: Children ages 3 and older. Targets on both vertical and horizontal surfaces, painted, and in the form of receptacles, such as wastebaskets, garbage cans, etc.; four or more balls of various sizes, ropes for additional targets, hoops, bean bags.

Description: First child throws ball in two or more targets in any order he chooses. Observing children must then throw the same ball in the same targets in the same order. Observing children check accuracy of second child.

Modifications: Targets may be added to and may assume an infinite number of varieties. Throwing implements may be varied— balls, bean bags, medicine balls, etc.

Demonstrating children may add to complexity by demonstrating numerous ways of throwing at same target (e.g., underhand, soft or hard throws, overhand) or at different targets; thus both the type of throw and the target employed must be remembered and replicated.

Implements may be varied for each target, so observing children may be asked to remember type of ball or other implement, sequence, and type of throw previous child executed.

GAME 13   Which Are Easier To Remember?

To Enhance: Short-term serial memory; awareness of which items of a series are easier to retain, and of methods of aiding serial memory.

Participants and Equipment: Children ages 8, 9, and older. Blackboard, playground equipment, mats, balls, ropes, configurations on ground (geometric figures made of tape).

Description: First demonstrating child shows a movement within each of five stations, i.e., configurations on ground, obstacles, etc. Observing children then, one by one, attempt to replicate movements at each of the stations. Observing children score which of the five items are successfully and unsuccessfully remembered by each of the performing children. Observing children should not be permitted to watch sometimes unsuccessful attempts of their predecessors, only the first attempt by the demonstrator.

32

Comparison is then made of which of the five movement "items" seems easiest to retain by the various children—was it one of the initial two movements, the last movement, or one of the intermediate movements, third or fourth?

Discussion should follow concerning possible results of the experiment—implications for listening, studying, remembering lessons, etc.

Modifications: More than five movements may be included, or a buildup of movements from two or three to more may be employed.

More than one scorer may be employed to check scoring accuracy and to give all scorers a chance to demonstrate possible serial-order effects.

Balls may be employed to make movements more interesting.

Theoretically, movements within the "middle" of the series are most difficult to remember and replicate; the effects of extra rehearsal of these intermediate items might be studied by the children.

GAME 14   Ten Times and Learning

To Enhance :   Awareness of the effects of practice upon memory.

Participants and Equipment :   Children ages 7 and older. Varied equipment : ropes, balls, hoops, boxes, chairs, tables, geometric configurations on ground ; blackboard.

NAME	1	2	3	4	5	6
JON	✗	O	O	✗	✗	O
GREG	✗	✗	✗	O	O	✗
SUE	✗		O	✗	✗	O
BETTE	✗					
CHRIS						
MARY						
LES						

Description: Demonstrator shows observing children, in a single demonstration, how to perform each of six separate movements. Then children, one at a time, atempt to replicate movements shown; scorekeeper records success of each child on the blackboard. Demonstrator shows group *between* each attempt to replicate movements, the six movements again, so that possible learning effects may be plotted by scorekeeper, comparing first child's attempts to replicate movements with last child's attempts.

Discussion should follow concerning practice effects upon individual performance, both in motor tasks and in mental-verbal tasks.

Modifications: Teams of three children each may be formed, one a demonstrator, the second a recorder, and the third a performer. Performer attempts, in successive trials interpolated by additional demonstrations, to perform a series of six, seven, or even eight movements. Demonstrator, recorder, and performer may rotate roles, using a new series of movements each time.

Comparisons may be made of the effects of demonstrations after every attempt to replicate versus after every second or third attempt to replicate efforts of the initial child demonstrating.

Older children, using graph paper, may plot individual or group performance curves, based upon successes during successive trials.

GAME 15   Interference

To Enhance: Concentration in the presence of distractions, short-term memory, intermediate-term memory, ability to mentally rehearse items in a series.

Participants and Equipment: Children ages 5 and older; retarded children ages 8, 9, and older. Variety of playground equipment, ropes, balls, hoops, etc.

Description: Initially a child demonstrates a series of four or five movements, while observers are told that they must remember and later duplicate these movements. Then a second child demonstrates a different series of five movements.

Observing children, one by one, are then asked to repeat the first series. Possible interfering effects of second series observed are discussed, with implications for concentration.

Modifications: Children may be asked to replicate movements contained in the second of two different series, with interfering effects discussed. Children may be asked to replicate a series of movements, with and without a second and different series of movements placed before or after the series to be remembered.

Memory of a movement series, with and without instructions to retain, may be compared in individual versus groups of children. Discussion of how people may concentrate differently when they know that they must later demonstrate retention of what they have been exposed to, might be held.

Second series may be quite similar in nature to, or different from series to be replicated. More than two series might be demonstrated, and observers may be asked to demonstrate first, second, or final series of movements. Comparisons of serial-order effects in retention may be discussed.

GAME 16   Hear, Tell, and Show

To Enhance: Appreciation of varieties of ways we learn and of which type of demonstration elicits best learning; short-term serial retention effects of various kinds of demonstrations.

Participants and Equipment: Children ages 7, 8, and older; retarded children ages 10 and older. Variety of playground equipment, obstacles, geometric configurations, etc.; blackboard, paper, cards.

Description: Children are divided into three groups; they are then exposed to a series of three or more movements, presented to each group in a different way: one, movements read to them from a card; two, demonstration of the same movements; three, both a demonstration and simultaneous verbal description of the movements.

Comparisons are then made of how well each group of observers demonstrates their retention via their replication of the movement series. Scorekeepers keep a tally, by item, of the number of successful replications of each group.

Discussion should follow of how various types of skills may be learned best, of individual differences in how people learn, and of how teachers may teach best for all children.

Modifications: Parts of a series may be presented in each of the three ways, e.g., first parts just read, intermediate parts both read and demonstrated, and final parts demonstrated.

Observer, recorder, and performer teams may be formed, rotating roles after initial performance and attempts at replication. Evaluators may check on the accuracy of verbal descriptions formulated by teachers or children.

A chain of communication may be formed, e.g., initial demonstration to a child, who must then change movements to words and then read them to a third child, who demonstrates to a fourth, who then must both demonstrate and verbalize to a fifth, etc. Final performance of the chain is then compared to initial performance by demonstrator.

GAME 17   The Next Day

To Enhance: Appreciation of elements that aid intermediate-term memory.

Participants and Equipment: Children ages 5 and older. Variety of playground equipment, obstacles, geometric configurations, etc.

Description: A series of four, five, or six movements is performed; on the following day, the observing children are asked to replicate movements seen the previous day.

Discussion of possible effects of mental rehearsal and effects of time lag between demonstration and replication should be held. Serial position effects should also be noted.

Scorekeepers determine how much is remembered, how many trials are necessary the next day to learn movement to perfection, and which of the elements in the series seem best retained.

Modifications: Series might be practiced to perfection the first day, and then one or more days allowed to elapse before reperformance. Comparison might be made of groups who receive instructions to retain versus groups who were given no instruction.

Forgetting curves might be plotted by older children over successive days, using same or different children on each day.

Time lapse of a week or more might be inserted between initial learning and replication.

Comparision of percent of the series retained by an individual or group could be made by contrasting initial learning to reperformance, or "savings" method could be employed to evaluate amount of retention (i.e., how many trials are necessary following retention interval to bring performance back to initial perfect level).

The following table appears on the chalkboard in the illustration:

second day	1	2	3		5	6
JOE	2	1	3		3	1
ANN	1	2			1	2
CHRIS						
PETE						
SUE						

GAME 18 Observation versus Practice

To Enhance: Appreciation of physical practice effects versus mental practice effects in learning and retention.

Participants and Equipment: Children ages 5, 6, and older; retarded children ages 7, 8, and older. Variety of playground equipment, ropes, balls, mats, etc.

Description: A demonstrator first shows a series of three, four, or more movements, which observing children may only watch, and then attempt to replicate after a five-minute time lag. Then demonstrator shows another series, which observing children may practice physically during five-minute interval prior to retest. Next, demonstrator shows a third series of movements, which observing children are asked to think about, and to practice "in their heads"; again replication is attempted after five minutes.

Comparisons are made, formally or informally, of the success of the replications after each condition. Discussions of the effects of direct physical practice upon academic skills and of the effects of mentally practicing skills should be carried out.

Modifications: Demonstrator, observer, performer, and evaluator teams may be formed, with participants rotating roles after each demonstration followed by each type of practice on the part of the performer.

Older children may plot performance curves after successive exposures to opportunities to mentally rehearse movements, practice movements, or simply observe movements.

BIBLIOGRAPHY

ADAMS, JACK A. *Human Memory.* New York: McGraw-Hill Book Company, 1967.

BERGES, J., and LEZINE, I. *The Imitation of Gestures.* London: The Spastics Society Medical Education and Information Unit in Association with William Heinemann Medical Books Ltd., 1965.

CRATTY, BRYANT J. *Active Learning.* Englewood Cliffs, N.J.: Prentice-Hall, Inc., 1971.

————. "Comparisons of Verbal-Motor Performance and Learning in Serial Memory Tasks," in *Research Quarterly* 34 (December 1963): 4.

————. *Human Behavior: Exploring Educational Processes.* Wolfe City, Texas: University Press, 1971.

————. "Recency Versus Primacy in a Complex Gross Motor Task," in *Research Quarterly* 34 (March 1963): 3–8.

————, and MARTIN, SISTER MARGARET MARY. *The Effects of a Program of Learning Games Upon Selected Academic Abilities in Children with Learning Difficulties.* Washington, D.C.: U.S. Office of Education, Bureau of Education for the Handicapped, 1971.

————; IKEDA, NAMIKO; MARTIN, SISTER MARGARET MARY; BENNETT, CLAIR; and MORRIS, MARGARET. *Movement Activities, Motor Ability and the Education of Children.* Springfield, Ill.: Charles C. Thomas, Publisher, 1970.

FROSTIG, MARIANNE, and MASLOW, PHYLLIS. *Movement Education: Theory and Practice.* Chicago: Follett Educational Corporation, 1970.

McCORMICK, CLARENCE; SCHNOBRICH, JANICE; and FOOTLIK, S. WILLARD. *Perceptual-Motor Training and Cognitive Achievement.* Downer's Grove, Ill.: George Williams College, 1967.

MILLER, GEORGE. "The Magical Number Seven, plus or minus two: Some Limits on our Capacity for Processing Information," in *Psychology Review* 63 (1966): 81–97.

NORMAN, DONALD A. *Memory and Attention.* New York: John Wiley & Sons, Inc., 1969.

UHR, LEONARD, ed. *Pattern Recognition.* New York: John Wiley & Sons, Inc., 1966.

three

CATEGORIZATION

Many typologies of intellectual functioning include abilities that involve making discriminations—placing objects, events, symbols, and so on into categories, and performing similar operations involving classification. The existence of this type of ability can be discerned in infants a few days old. For example, it has been found that infants evidence the inclination to spend more time visually inspecting unfamiliar or unusual stimuli than watching familiar faces and shapes within close proximity. Additionally, T.G. Bower and her colleagues have found that infants of from 40 to 60 days of age can discern differences in two-dimensional and three-dimensional shapes, and can apparently discriminate between similar objects placed at different distances away. Thus, during the first months of birth, infants have been shown to be able to categorize simple stimuli in various rudimentary ways.

As the infant matures, the ability to make more complex discriminations, to place objects, people, and events into increasingly discrete categories, are important criteria upon which to base assessments of intellectual functioning. By the time the child reaches school, he must not only discriminate among the various letter shapes in the alphabet, but must also recognize characteristics common to the 26 letters even though they may appear in different sizes, print styles, and location within his space field. If his efforts at reading are to be successful, he must also categorize word shapes into innumerable categories representing a multitude of meanings.

Based on his tests of children from two years of age and older, Piaget suggests that the ability to classify passes through three stages of development:

1. The preoperational stage (2 to 5 years) is the one in which children evidence difficulty placing geometric figures or representations of objects into "pure" categories. Often a "partial alignment" with some objects which are similar will be formed by the child during this age span.

2. In the second stage (5 to 7), children produce collections which seem to be true and valid classes. In one study, for example, children were seen by Piaget to arrange objects into two large categories, one containing all the polygons and the other containing curvilinear forms. Moreover, these same children could divide these categories further, placing all triangles in one pile and the rectangles in a second, while the curvilinear forms were similarly divided into those which included rings and those which were half-rings.

3. The third stage (about 7 to 11 years) is marked by the ability to construct reasonably complex hierarchical classifications and to comprehend the qualities reflected by objects which determine their arrangement into various groups. Thus, for example, pictures of flowers can be separated from pictures of plants; furthermore, the pictures of flowers can be divided into those of various types, while finally those within each name grouping may be further divided into those of various colors.

Movements and their meanings and uses must similarly be categorized by the growing child. Diffuse and discoordinate actions in the neonate become refined and specialized to meet life's many exigencies. Moreover, these actions must become paired with verbal meanings, which may be voiced silently and inwardly or put forth by others.

The various programs of education in which movement plays a

part have not contained a great many types of tasks which could conceivably enhance the child's ability to classify and to categorize. Those tasks which have appeared in the various programs might fall into the following categories:

1. Practice in pattern recognition constitutes the first category, in which various movement games and motor responses are encouraged, with the use of large geometric figures placed on the playground. The attempt here seems to be to aid children to place verbal labels on commonly seen geometric figures. These types of activities are designed to enhance the classification and categorization of what Guilford would term "figural content."

2. The letter-recognition activities described in other publications, particularly if a wide range of transfer is taught (for example, identifying lower case, upper case, written letter, spoken letter, letter sound, etc.), represent another attempt through movement experiences to aid a child to form categories into which letters and letter combinations might be "placed."

3. In programs of movement education a child may be asked to perform a movement within a given category, but at the same time may be permitted some latitude in his exact choice of movement. For example, an instructor may ask a child to "move down the mat a backwards way," or to "show me a hopping way to get into the hoop." Within this context a child is being encouraged to form categories of movement experiences and to demonstrate his acquisition of various categorical concepts by describing various actions with his own body, or by observing and judging the efforts of another child to describe the same types of behaviors. These exercises are thus designed to enhance the classification of *behavioral content*.

4. Various spatial concepts may be learned through movement experiences seen in several programs. A child may, for example, be asked to do "something to the left" or "with the left side of your body," or may be asked to go under or over a chair or other obstacle to purportedly enhance acquisition of the spatial concepts of up-down and left-right. For instance, division of movements into four categories, corresponding to up-down and left-right, may be used.

5. Most of the reading games presented by Cratty and Humphrey might be considered to be practice in categorization. A word shape (such as "look") must be classified, compared to other similar but different word shapes and word sounds, and in other ways categorized in order to be truly learned. Specifically, Hum-

phrey lists two games in his text *Teaching Slow Learners Through Active Games* which purportedly enhance the ability to classify letters; one involves arranging pictures of various kinds of animals (classifiable according to type, like "fish," or to function, "can fly"), the children running to place the correct pictures in various cages without being caught by other participants. A second game, "Ducks Fly," is similar in purpose.

The data emerging from the programs in which these activities have a part are not extensive. However, in a study we carried out in which one of the objectives was to enhance children's verbal identification of geometric patterns (circle, square, half-circle, rectangle, and triangle), it was found that using a total-body movement approach was as successful as attempting to ingrain the same categorical concepts via small-group tutoring in a classroom environment.

The games which follow sample a rather broad spectrum of tasks which require thought about categories. The broad classifications seen in most of the games involve either the classification of movements themselves, or the classification of visual symbols, made vivid by the ancillary incorporation of motor acts.

GAME 1   Triangle Things

To Enhance: Perception of conceptual differences and similarities within and between common geometric figures; ability to place verbal labels in categories of commonly seen shapes.

Participants and Equipment: From 2 to 30 children, ages 3-6 years. Lining tape, cardboard, scissors, blackboard, mats.

Description: The teacher should announce that the purpose of the lesson is to discover all the "triangle" things we can do. Thus, after hearing a description of what a triangle is, and using the materials available, the children should be encouraged to cut triangles out of cardboard, mark out triangles of large dimensions with the tape, make "triangles" with the limbs, fingers, or bodies, either on a horizontal or vertical plane.

Modifications: Lesson may be modified to include any common geometric figure—squares, circles, rectangles, diamonds, etc.

Further discussion may transpire as to differences and similarities between triangles and other configurations.

The configurations, once placed on the playground, may be used for base games of various kinds.

Children may be asked to run to the nearest triangle, whether on the playground, on the blackboard, cut out of cardboard, etc.

Children may be asked how they can change common geometric figures into letter shapes, e.g., half-circles to B's, triangles into A's. They may then be asked to demonstrate these changes, by changing their body positions, changing the tape on the playground, changing the lines on the blackboard.

GAME 2   Look and Select

To Enhance: Ability to categorize movements; ability to determine if items belong in more than one category and to place them correctly; sharp observations of game activity; awareness of own movement abilities in games.

Participants and Equipment: Children ages 7, 8, and older. Various kinds of equipment as needed; balls, bases, courts, etc.

	2 FEET	1 FOOT
RUNNING	x x x x x	x x x
JUMPING	x x x x x	
DRIBBLING	x x x	
STOPPING	x x x x x	
SHOOTING	x x x	x

Description: The object of this exercise is to observe a game, such as basketball, and then to classify all the types of movements which are seen in the game: running, jumping from two feet, jumping from one foot, running and jumping, dribbling forward, dribbling and stopping, shooting with two hands, with one hand, with one hand while jumping, etc.

Next, children may be asked to demonstrate the various components, and then to place components into categories, making sure that first more global categories are devised—perhaps vertical versus horizontal movement, or ball movement versus people movement only—and then placing movements or skills seen into more discrete categories.

Modifications: Children might be asked to determine which movements in a given game are exclusive to that game and which are seen in other games, either in similar or identical form.

Children might be asked to collect movements from several games and invent a new game composed of these movements.

Children might be asked to classify how people act when playing games—mad, happy, vocal, nonvocal—and to determine whether the game causes the characteristic seen, or whether the people's personalities emerge in the games; and whether the behavior is specific to the game or to the position or situation in which the players find themselves.

GAME 3   Up and Down Things

To Enhance: Ability to perceive common characteristics of up and down movements, lines, and their relationship to components of letter and number forms.

Participants and Equipment: Pre-school children, retarded children ages 6 and older. Butcher paper, blackboards, playground equipment, ropes, paper, and pencils.

Description: Following discussion of what does up and down each as elevators, airplanes, helicopters, children go to playground to determine what they can see or do which also goes up or down, such as sliding down pole, jumping up in the air, climbing and coming down a rope, etc.

Next the children go to the classroom, and using large movements of their arms, draw up and down movements on the blackboard or on butcher paper arranged vertically on a wall. Green balls at the top may signal "start" while red balls at the end may signify "stop."

Finally the children go to the paper on a desk, and make up and down lines, in series—first vertically, or in a slanted plane, and then horizontally—emphasizing that *up* now means away from the body while *down* means toward the body.

Modifications: Up and down playground activities may be drawn on the blackboard or on paper. Up and down lines may be changed into common objects, such as houses or trees, either on the larger paper or on the desk-top paper.

Children may return to playground to check on other things that go up and down, after their writing practice.

GAME 4 Slanted Things

To Enhance: Perceptions of slanted lateral lines, and general characteristics of these lines, and of the movements which produce them; awareness of the manner in which slanted lines aid in the production of letter and number shapes.

Participants and Equipment: Children ages 3, 4, and older; retarded children ages 6, 7, and older. Ropes, sliding board, teeter-totter, climbing apparatus, sticks.

Description: Following a discussion and demonstration of slanted things, children go to playground and attempt to observe, and to experience via their own movements, "slanted" movements within the playground context—sliding down a sliding board, climbing an inclined bar, holding a rope in a slanted position and jumping over it, etc.

Next, children go to large blackboards or large sheets of paper placed on either horizontal or vertical surfaces, and attempt, with limb movements, to reproduce slanted lateral lines.

Finally the children move to small desk-size paper and make slanted lines, slanted both lower left to upper right and vice versa, and show how these lines may be used to make pictures, such as slanted roofs, as well as various letters.

Modifications: Children may also search in their environment for slanted lines, e.g., hillsides, lines, etc.

Children may experiment with varying degrees of "slantedness" as they draw. Drawings of slanted lines may be alternated with drawings of horizontal and vertical lines in order to illustrate similarities and differences.

GAME 5   Curved Things

To Enhance: Ability to detect and replicate curved lines of various magnitudes, from line segments to completed circles to multiple circles and S shapes; ability to discriminate between curved and straight lines and movements.

Participants and Equipment: Preschool children; retarded children ages 6, 7, and older. Circles on the playground, ropes, balls, etc.

Description: Children, using lines on the playground, observing the flight of balls or how ropes hang when held at each end, attempt to find as many curved things as they can during a play period. Walking varying distances around a circle on the playground, for example, is a curved thing.

Next the children draw curved lines on the blackboard, on paper placed on the floor, or on other appropriate large surfaces.

Finally the curves are placed in various ways on a page, while the children are seated at a desk; and then the curves are incorporated into letters which require curves, or into pictures containing curved lines.

Modifications: Children might try to replicate curved lines by placing spin on balls as they release them; they might experiment drawing or reproducing, via gross movement patterns, curves within various planes and of varying degrees of curvature.

GAME 6 Left Things and Up Things

To Enhance: Concepts relative to left-right and up-down spatial dimensions.

Participants and Equipment: Children ages 5 and older; retarded children ages 7 and older, as able. Blackboard, balls, ropes, hoops, tape for lining floor or cement outdoor area.

Description: Demonstration is made of a movement, such as jumping on the left foot. Discussion is then held as to what was just done. When it is discovered by some child that the jump was made on the left foot, the children then using all the equipment available attempt to do other "left things."

Next a movement, such as turning, is done to the right. After discussion again, children are encouraged to do many kinds of "right things."

Same strategy is employed to inculcate up things and down things.

Modifications: Up things, down things, and left and right things are done on a blackboard, after first determining which is the left, right, up, and down of the board. *Note:* Usually the easiest left-right things will involve using the hands or feet. More difficult is being able, when asked, to turn to the right or left. Most difficult is orienting the body with relation to something else, e.g., stand with your right side nearest the wall; or lie down so that your left arm is on the floor.

Further left-right and up-down practice may be attempted with letters and numbers, opening either to the left or right, or having their round part to the left or right. Next, left and right letters may be made with the children's bodies or limbs forming the letters, with observing children checking the results.

GAME 7   Intersecting Things

To Enhance: Ability to cross lines, and cross curves with lines, without becoming confused; ability to categorize lines which intersect, and to relate them to letters which require intersecting lines.

Participants and Equipment: Children ages 3, 4, and older; retarded children ages 6 to 8 and older. Blackboard, paper of various sizes, playground with circles and lines painted on it, ropes, hoops, sticks.

Description: Using climbing apparatus and lines on playground, children should try to find intersecting lines, and to either climb or walk them in various ways.

Next, children may return to large blackboard, or paper placed on floor or vertically, and draw intersecting lines of various types. Finally, using small paper on a desk top, children should try to draw lines intersecting in various ways, and to form these lines into letters and numerals which require intersecting lines.

Modifications: Designs and pictures containing intersecting lines may be drawn. Games which require intersecting lines may be invented.

Children may try to classify letters and numbers into two categories, those which require intersecting lines and those which do not.

GAME 8   Lines and Circles

To Enhance: Ability to classify, and to substitute one classification system for another; movement to visual symbol translations.

Participants and Equipment: Children ages 3 and older. Blackboards, mats.

Description: The "code" is first explained: / on the blackboard represents a single hop (on one foot). Thus when two //'s are written, two hops must be taken, etc. The children should demonstrate.

Next the code is expanded to include 0's, which represent two-foot jumps. Thus 00 written on the blackboard means two jumps using both feet at the same time.

Next the code is combined. Thus the children may be asked to "read" and perform what //0/ means, for example, with combinations of increasing length.

Next the symbols may be broken up for clarity. Thus // 0/ 0/ /0 may be placed on the board, over the same symbols placed close together, //0/0//0. Children are asked to state differences in these two lines—that is, one group has spaces—and to act them out.

Next, children may be asked what they might do to indicate spaces shown in the first grouping above. Expected answers: "wait," or "pause," or perhaps "make a noise or clap" to indicate space, or maybe even do each combination in a different place, that is, use "space to represent space."

Modifications: Additional movements may be paired with additional symbols, thus extending the code: an "x" may mean a front roll on the mat, while a "d" might stand for "fall down." With little extension, the abstraction "j-u-m-p" (abstract to a four-year-old) may be acted out by jumping! In this way bright young children or less capable older children may be encouraged to read—itself a coding process.

GAME 9 Footprints

To Enhance: Ability to code and decode; ability to form categories across sensory modalities, e.g., visual to motor; ability to make left-right discriminations.

Participants and Equipment: Three or more children, ages 5 and older. A set of 18 footprints, 9 forming left feet and colored a dark color, and 9 a light color shaped like the right foot; a mat or clean floor area.

Description: Footprints are placed in a line in random order, while children are instructed that the dark footprints are the left foot and the light ones are the right foot.

The children then are asked to walk, hop, or jump down the footprints in any manner they wish, keeping their feet on the proper footprints.

They may attempt to determine how many ways they can come down the row of prints. Another child may wish to arrange the prints in another way.

Modifications: Children may use footprints which are placed increasing distances apart.

An increasing number of prints may be employed; or prints may be placed in increasingly complex ways, e.g., some facing the starting point, requiring the child to execute half turns.

GAME 10 Into How Many Categories?

To Enhance: Ability to analyze, to separate action into innumerable categories.

Participants and Equipment: Children ages 5-10. Rope, mat or clean floor, blackboard.

START

Description: Demonstrator (teacher or child) executes a movement, such as hopping backwards along a line six times with the left foot.

Teacher then asks, "How many ways can you describe what has been done?" or "How many single words would be needed to describe that to someone who has not seen it?" *Possible answers:* backwards, hopping, a one-foot movement, a rhythmic movement, a straight-line movement, a backwards movement, a left movement, a foot movement, a six-count movement.

After each answer, the children are asked to perform the movement described.

Modifications: Using a blackboard, the children may be encouraged to write down the categories arrived at and then list other possible variations within each category.

Using a blackboard, a child might be asked to do other similar things (e.g., six things,) using only a chalk and a blackboard, when possible.

Innumerable other complex movements might be done initially—e.g., four front rolls, hopping with a half turn over a line, running and stopping, etc.—with the same discussion, classification, and confirmation via movement to follow, as outlined above.

GAME 11   What Is a Game?

To Enhance: Processes of analysis and classification relative to the qualities of various cultural activities, such as games, religions, jobs, recreation, fighting, etc.

Participants and Equipment: Children ages 5 and older. Playground equipment, balls, ropes, hoops, etc.; mats.

Description: Discussion of what qualities are seen in games e.g., what do games need, what happens when you play a game, etc. *Possible answers:* Games require space, one or more than one person, rules, equipment; they involve fun, movement, trying hard, etc.

Next, children are asked to invent a game which has never been played before, or are exposed to a game which is new to them or one which they have played before. After being permitted to demonstrate the game, they are asked about each component identified above in relation to the game: How is space used in your game? What rules does your game have? What movement is seen in your game? etc.

Modifications: Two simple games may be combined into a complex game and analyzed according to written criteria.

Discussion may ensue as to which qualities are absolutes in games, and which are seen in only some games and not in others. Various other classification scales along which games may be considered could also be discussed, and then acted out through movement, e.g., the degree to which speed is required, the degree to which complexity of movement is required, the degree to which direct versus indirect contact with opponents is required.

Extremes in game qualities might be attempted; play a game in the smallest or largest space you can imagine, play a game with a minimum of rules or a great many rules, play a game with no equipment or with a great deal of equipment, etc.

GAME 12   A's Are a's . . .

To Enhance: Ability to generalize letter shape seen in various forms.

Equipment: Upper and lower case letters, some movable, some on cards, some fixed on grids; blackboard.

Description: Innumerable transfer games may be played including the following: from written lower case letter, find the upper case equivalent on grid by jumping into it.

Written letters presented via cards may be found in a pile of upper case letters, as children see who can run to the pile and pick up appropriate letter first.

Children may be asked to spell out word, seen via lower case letters, jumping into upper case equivalents.

Modifications: Given a letter auditorily, children can find all possible forms of the letter, via jumping, running and finding it in a pile of others, etc.

Children can be asked to give letter phonically when it is presented visually in the various possible forms.

GAME 13 Types of Letter Shapes

To Enhance: Awareness of letter shapes and of the categories into which letters may be placed relative to their shapes; ability to identify letter shapes of upper and lower case letters.

Participants and Equipment: Children 3-7 years. Mats, blackboard, school yard with configurations as shown in illustration, movable cards containing upper and lower case letters.

Description: Using the blackboard, children may be asked to classify upper case letters according to "shape" categories, i.e., those which are circular and continuous (C, O, S); those which have slanted lines and straight lines (A, K, M, N, V, W, X, Y, Z); those which have both curved and straight portions (B, D, G, J, P, Q, R, U); those which have only horizontal or vertical straight lines (E, F, H, I, L, T).

Then children may be asked to position their bodies in the proper positions for each one, or to jump into a playground maze containing letters of each type, as shown, or to run and collect letters of each type from a pile of movable letters.

Modifications: Using their hands, limbs, and bodies, children may be asked to replicate letters of various kinds while standing vertically. They may be asked to walk through the letter shapes in a sandbox, or perhaps be asked to draw large and small letter shapes of various kinds on large pieces of paper on the floor or on the blackboard.

Only a multi-dimensional line may be employed on the playground, with the children required to place proper letters (upper or lower case) on cards, at proper points on the line.

BIBLIOGRAPHY

BOWER, T. G. "The Visual World of Infants," *Scientific American* 215 (1966), 80–97.

CRATTY, BRYANT J. *Active Learning.* Englewood Cliffs, N.J.: Prentice-Hall, Inc., 1971.

————. "Visual Perceptual Development," in *Perceptual and Motor Development in Infants and Children.* New York: The Macmillan Company, 1970.

GUILFORD, J. P. *Intelligence, Creativity, and their Educational Implications.* San Diego, Calif.: Robert R. Knapp, Publisher, 1968.

HUMPHREY, JAMES H., and SULLIVAN, DOROTHY D. *Teaching Slow Learners Through Active Games.* Springfield, Ill.: Charles C. Thomas, Publisher, 1970.

MILLER, GEORGE; GALANTER, EUGENE; and PRIBRAM, KARL. *Plans and the Structure of Behavior.* New York: Holt, Rinehart & Winston, Inc., 1960.

PARNES, S. J. *Student Workbook for Creative Problem-Solving Courses and Institutes.* Buffalo, N.Y.: State University of New York at Buffalo, 1961.

PIAGET, JEAN. *The Origins of Intelligence in Children,* translated by M. Cook. New York: International University Press, 1952.

UHR, LEONARD, ed. *Pattern Recognition.* New York: John Wiley & Sons, Inc., 1966.

UPTON, A., and SAMSON, R. W. *Creative Analysis.* New York: E. P. Dutton & Co., Inc., 1963.

four

LANGUAGE

COMMUNICATION

Language, speech, reading, and motor activity interact in both obvious and subtle ways. Speech itself is to some degree a motor act, and it is common to find a relatively larger percentage of speech problems in groups of youth who evidence other signs of motor dysfunction. Likewise, to some degree speech therapy involves encouraging the child to perceive the manner in which mouth, tongue, and lip movements must correctly manifest themselves in the formation of sounds within the culturally sanctioned language.

Motor activity and communication also coalesce when various kinds of gesture and movement cues accompany the spoken word. The popular press, as well as articles appearing in scientific journals, have increasingly begun to explore the parameters of nonverbal speech, much of which involves movement cues eminating from the face, the limbs, and the trunk of the "sender."

From a developmental standpoint, one may pair movement and speech. No less an authority than Piaget suggests that the earliest appearance of language understanding occurs in children in connection with movement activities. Before he is able to formulate language himself, the infant learns to respond correctly to various parental commands to move or to stop moving. Shortly after his first birthday he can carry out such commands as "Stop that!" "Bring it here," "Come here," "Let's see you run," and similar verb phrases denoting an action or a cessation of action.

While it could be argued that reading involves movement only of the smaller eye muscles, by middle and late childhood written communication demands movement accuracy of the hands. It also expresses sub-vocal speech, as a child first attempts to write a story.

Most interesting, however, are recent attempts to prompt various kinds of language development through the use of bodily activities involving some of the larger muscle groups. This research has produced findings indicating that various kinds of motor activities, when paired with certain kinds of verbal communication, generally result in improvement of the latter abilities. These findings, together with the clinical practices which produced them, will be discussed in this chapter.

There have been several approaches to enhancing language functions, reading, and written communication through programs involving movement tasks. For example:

1. The "active games" approach has been used to instill language concepts in normal children. In one approach of this nature the rules of the game are written and discussed prior to playing the game, with the language lesson and the game taking place at separate times.

2. Foreign languages have been learned by pairing commands in the language with what has been termed "the total physical response," much as is done when young children learn their own language or a foreign tongue.

3. A number of authors have incorporated prereading competencies into activities which involve hopping, jumping, and similar locomotor activities. Such basic abilities as letter recognition (by sight and by sound), pattern recognition, and serial memory ability have been the focus of this type of program.

4. Sight-reading exercises have been incorporated directly into

games, with children moving from base to base, for example, after correctly identifying words on flash cards.

The use of this type of approach to language development has been justified in several ways. Some authors suggest that games are highly motivating to children, and when paired with language skills of various kinds are likely to "spread" their motivating effects to the often oppressive learning of reading and similar skills.

Others have implied that the abundance of kinesthetic input occurring as a child moves and learns various language skills aids in the formation of reading and other communication concepts. Still others have implied that a kind of imprinting involving language skills is enhanced by pairing the total physical response with some kind of communication training.

In any case, the findings from some of these studies are quite provocative and have several types of implications for the teaching of various communication skills.

There are types of movement activities which, if properly employed, may make a contribution to improving some of the subprocesses needed in order for some children to read well. The material that follows *should not* be interpreted to mean that one should reject some of the more traditional ways of teaching reading, many of which have served children extremely well during the past decades. At the same time, reference to the games contained in the following pages may encourage some teachers to approach some children in ways that are new and creative, and thus may penetrate to the child who is difficult to teach.

The following processes are usually agreed upon by most reading experts as valid ones, although there is often controversy as to the *order* in which they should be acquired.[1]

1. The child must speak and understand the language to a reasonable skill level before he learns to read.

2. The child must learn to dissect spoken words into component sounds.

3. The child must learn to recognize and discriminate the vari-

---

[1] These processes have been taken from a paper by John B. Carroll, Ph.D., which appears in a collection of reference papers from a Reading Forum sponsored by the National Institute of Neurological Diseases and Stroke, under the National Institutes of Health and the U.S. Department of Education. Other papers in this collection are excellent and should be reviewed by educators interested in various facets of teaching reading. It may be ordered from the Superintendent of Documents, U.S. Government Printing Office, Washington, D.C. 20402, for $2.00 (NINDS Monograph #11).

ous letter forms to which he is exposed (lower case, upper case, manuscript, etc.).

4. The child must learn the left-right principle by which letters and words are ordered in a continuous text.

5. The child must learn that various sounds are probable outcomes of various letter combinations, so that he may either recognize in print words that are commonly heard, or conversely, so that he can attempt to pronounce words seen for the first time.

6. The child must learn to recognize printed words by referring to a number of cues, their general shape, the letters composing them, the sounds the letters represent, and also the meanings suggested by their context.

7. The child must be able to translate spoken words and phrases to written words and phrases, and vice versa.

8. The child must learn to reason and to think about what is read, to the limits of his capacity and talent.

There are numerous valid strategies and methods which have been found effective in the teaching of reading and in the remediation of reading problems, most of which exclude a great deal of movement on the part of the child. The games on the following pages, however, contain strategies in which the child is most of the time encouraged to move in various ways.

GAME 1   Do What I Say

To Enhance: Communication via language, language comprehension, expressive language.

Participants and Equipment: Children ages 3 and older, normal or retarded. Chairs, tables, hoops, balls, ropes.

Description: Lay out a course composed of a table, chair, hoop, and rope placed in a line. A "directing" child describes, in sequence, what a performing child should do, e.g., sit on the chair, go under the table, jump into the hoop, etc. An observing child attempts to determine whether directions have been carried out correctly.

Child performing correctly may then make up the next series of directions. Verbal directors, performers, and evaluators rotate roles periodically.

Modifications: A chain of children can be formed, with the first child making up directions and whispering them to a second child, who may whisper them to a third, and so on, until final child repeats them to the performer. Evaluator (who also hears directions from first child) determines the accuracy of the final result as compared to first directions given.

An increasing number of complex directions can be given to the performer.

Variations of tempo can be introduced, e.g., do something slowly, fast, etc.

Time delays of varying lengths may be inserted between the directions and the performance, to enhance short-term memory and to encourage mental rehearsal.

GAME 2   Watch, Listen, and Retell

To Enhance: Ability to observe, communicate verbally, communicate accurately; visual and auditory short-term memory.

Participants and Equipment: Children ages 4 and older, with or without communication problems. Lining tape, boxes, hoops, balls, ropes.

Description: Place configurations on floor, as shown, or with modifications using lining tape. Have children seated in groups of two, one facing toward and the other facing away from the configurations. A demonstrating child does one or more "things" to one or more configurations, e.g., hops, walks around, etc.

Children facing configurations must then tell their partner, who was not permitted to watch, what the demonstrator did. Confirmation of the accuracy of communication takes place when children who were told what was done attempt to replicate movement or movements.

Children who explain most accurately, or who perform best, can be next demonstrator. Children rotate from telling to performing roles.

Modifications: Child can tell a second child, who in turn tells a third child, prior to replicating.

Demonstrator can do more than one thing to an increasing number of configurations, making the remembering problem more difficult. Evaluators can confirm accuracy of replicated movement.

Three-dimensional obstacle course can be substituted for part or all of the taped course shown—tires, boxes, ladders, towers, etc.

GAME 3   The Robot

To Enhance: Listening skills, language comprehension, short-term visual memory, and short-term auditory memory; ability to follow directions.

Participants and Equipment: Five or more children, ages 4 or 5 and older. Room containing chairs, tables, hoops, etc.

Description: Five children are designated as "teller," "robot," one who can hear teller but who cannot see robot, one who can neither hear teller nor see robot, and one who cannot hear teller (fingers in ears) but who can see robot.

First teller tells robot to make a series of movements, with his total body and/or his limbs—e.g., left arm to your head, walk slowly to the chair—with the robot making stiff mechanical-like movements.

Then numerous problems may be presented to the children. For example:

Robot may be asked to repeat his movements in order.

Robot may be asked to tell child out of sight and hearing what he did.

Child permitted only to see demonstration may be asked to repeat movements.

Child permitted only to hear directions of teller may be asked to repeat movements in order.

After one or more of the above activities is engaged in and an evaluator has checked accuracy, children may change roles.

Modifications: Robot may be an animal going through the forest and doing various things. Robot may be asked to do an increasing number of activities which become increasingly complex.

Children may be asked to write down what they will tell robot, or what they see robot do, or what they hear robot being told, and then repeat their written directions for another robot, directions which may be checked for accuracy.

GAME 4   Break Up and Put Together Words

To Enhance: Analysis of word sounds, synthesis of sounds into total word, matching of sounds to letter and letter combinations; ability to break down words into syllables; analysis and synthesis of words.

Participants and Equipment: From 4 to 40 children, ages 4 and older. Grid containing either upper or lower case letters as shown, cards with upper or lower case letters on them, and/or large movable squares, each containing a single upper or lower case letter; blackboard.

Description: Two- or three-syllable words are spoken by the teacher. Children must then break down the words into component parts, using the grid, by jumping into first-syllable letters, hesitating, and then jumping into the letter or letters that make up middle or last syllable.

Children may be placed into relay lines; then one from each team is asked to run to a pile of letters, after first hearing or seeing a word, and see who is quicker at placing letters into proper syllable combinations.

Using the grid, children may be asked to jump into the letter or letters which give the word its first sound (e.g., in "jump," the letter J), which letter or letter combinations give the word its final sound (P), or in the case of more complex words, which letter or letters give the word its "middle sound" (in the case of "jump," the letters U and M).

Modifications: Children may be formed into teams, with a "teacher," evaluator, and one or more jumpers—the teacher giving a word, and the evaluator assessing the accuracy of the jumpers in dividing the word into component parts.

Child may be given the sound "parts" of a word out of order and asked to arrange them into proper order to form a word. Or he may be asked to search for other ways in which the same sounds may be put together.

Children may be asked to match different first sounds with various endings, by jumping into the proper "first sound" letter on the grid, i.e., what first sounds go with *un*, *at*, *ate*, etc.

GAME 5   Upper Case, Lower Case

To Enhance: Ability to categorize letter shapes appearing in several forms: written, lower case, upper case; classification ability, ability to transfer, to recognize common characteristics in letter shapes, to make discriminations between letters.

Participants and Equipment: Five or more children, ages 5 and older. Grids containing upper and lower case letters as shown, cards containing upper and lower case letters, or large squares (1' × 1') containing upper and lower case letters; blackboard.

Description: Children may play "find the letter," searching for all forms of a given letter, such as D. Children may be encouraged to write all forms of the letter on the blackboard, to jump in all

forms of the letter on the grids, and to find all forms of the letter in the various stacks of cards.

Using their bodies on the mat, either lying down or standing, children may be asked to change their shapes from a lower case to an upper case letter; observing children may attempt to "read" letter shapes as they are given and changed. Children may use trunks, limbs, and hands and fingers when forming letters.

Using a blacktop or floor area, a child may be asked to run through a letter shape in written form. Observing children may then attempt to guess the letter, write it on the board, or see who may first jump into the corresponding letter on the grid.

Modifications: More than one letter may be presented, the children then copying the series, translating from upper to lower case, to written form, etc.

Child may be asked to inscribe written letter in the air, using his finger as a pointer. Observing children, either facing him or within the same visual reference system (facing in the same direction as the "writer"), then try to guess letter and to replicate other forms of the letter found in the grids, stacks of cards, etc.

GAME 6   Left and Right

To Enhance: Awareness of the left-right principle by which letters in words are arranged, and by which words in sentences are ordered; categorization of spatial reference points, via left-right orientation.

Participants and Equipment: Children ages 5, 6, and older. Grids, hoops, cards or large squares containing letters, cards containing printed words.

Description: First a number of left-right games are played with children: finding left-right body parts is easiest, next placing things to the left and right of the body, and then relocating the left and right of the body relative to the environment (e.g., "lie down on your right side," "place your left side against the wall," etc.).

After these tasks are accomplished accurately, the children may be asked to jump into the left line of letters on the grid, then into the letters to the right of the grid. Now, facing a blackboard, they may be asked to find the left side of the board, then the right side of the board, then do the same task using a paper, book, and line of print.

Now letters are placed in front of them on the blackboard, some of them oriented correctly relative to the left-right reference system, others reversed. Children may be asked to jump into grid letters which are placed incorrectly (i.e., reversed)on the blackboard.

Modifications: Relays may be played, with an effort made to see which team can straighten out a séntence composed of individual words placed on cards.

A child holds a stack of cards containing letters, some of which may be reversed. He attempts to match letters with the correct letters on the grids by jumping into the latter. When he encounters a reversed letter on the card, he should be asked to put it aside, and correct it on the blackboard later.

GAME 7   Words and Sounds

To Enhance: Translation of letter combinations to probable sounds; awareness that certain letter combinations will likely stand for certain sounds; ability to "sound out" new letter combinations and new words.

Participants and Equipment: Six or more children, ages 6 and older. Letter grids, cards containing words, larger squares containing lower case letters, blackboard.

Description: One child jumps into letter grids at random. Letters contacted are placed in order on the blackboard. Observing children

then try to pronounce nonsense word produced. Teacher may have to insert vowels within the nonsense word.

Using a common word ending such as *ing*, *tion*, *ed*, etc., children try to compose beginnings of the words by jumping into letters on the grid. Discussion may ensue as to whether words produced are "real" ones or not.

Words may be given verbally, and then children, by jumping into letter grid, may attempt to produce the letter combinations which could represent the sound. Words with which the children are familiar should be attempted first, and then later words which are unfamiliar to the children may be employed.

Modifications: Children may search for all possible combinations of letters which could result in a certain sound or sounds—by jumping in grid, or by locating letters in a pile via a relay situation.

Complex words are spoken with and without an attempt made to separate them into syllables. Children then attempt to replicate them via some physical response, while separating them into syllables.

GAME 8   Observe, Write, and Read

To Enhance: Written and verbal communication.

Participants and Equipment: Children ages 7, 8, and older. Variety of playground equipment: balls, hoops, ropes, sticks, bats, etc.

bounce ball in hoop
hit ball with bat
run to base

Description: One team invents game; second team watches game, writes out rules which are apparent in the game, and then reads them to a third group, who has not had the opportunity to observe the first group play the game. Comparison of game as played by first group versus characteristics of game played by third group is made by evaluators.

Team or individuals designated as players, writers, and replayers rotate positions after each game is played, written about, read, and replayed.

Modifications: Game rules are written after discussion with first group, or without discussion, i.e., based solely upon inspection.

Two groups watching game independently write up rules as observed, and then compare written versions of the game.

GAME 9   Add On, and Say

To Enhance: Written communication, ability to synthesize and simplify information and discover relationships of games to cultures.

Participants and Equipment: Children ages 8 and older. Equipment as needed in game.

Description: Starting with a simple movement, one child demonstrates an action, with or without a piece of apparatus, while a second child observes. The second child then attempts either to describe verbally what occurred, or to write a description of what the first child did. Then the first child adds a component to the first movement demonstrated, and the second child again either describes it verbally or tries to write a description. This continues until finally the first child begins a simple game with a third child, and the observing child once more tries to write or to describe verbally what has occurred.

Modifications: Evaluating children attempt to determine the accuracy of the verbal or written description of what has occurred. Children who have not had the opportunity to see the first game must perform, basing their actions entirely on the verbal or written description eminating from the observing child or children. Performers, observers, and evaluators periodically rotate roles.

Score may be kept, with higher scores going to the children who can remember or describe games of increasing complexity. Movement can be changed into complex movement, complex movement into simple two- or three-child game, while simple game may be made more complex.

GAME 10 Games in Foreign Lands

To Enhance: Written communication; ability to synthesize and analyze games from foreign countries; ability to appreciate games from foreign lands, and to compare their cultural characteristics with native games.

Participants and Equipment: Children ages 7, 8, and older; retarded children ages 10 and older. Variety of playground equipment, special equipment for foreign games as needed.

Description: Children formed into two- or three-member teams engage in library research to discover what games are played in foreign lands. The rules of these games may be written out and explained verbally and in written form to other class members, who can then practice them. Each team of researchers presents game in turn to rest of the class.

82

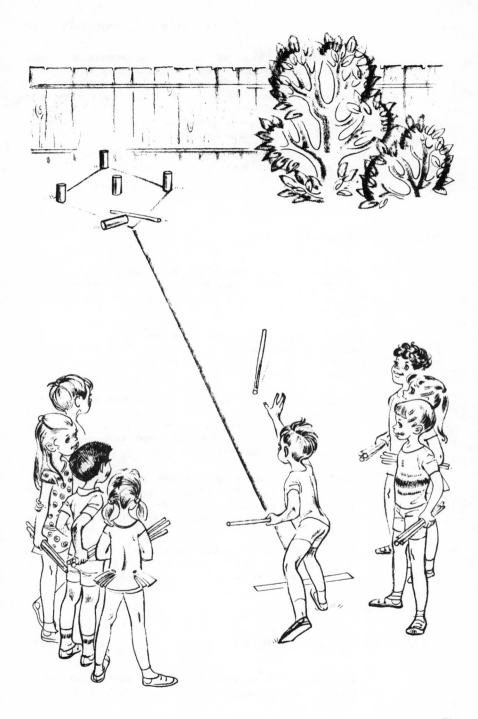

Modifications: More able children can attempt to analyze national characteristics with regard to games played by children in a given country. Games can be described, and then other children may guess from which country the game has emerged. Games from foreign lands may be compared to similar games from the United States. "Families" of games from around the world can be collected and analyzed for similar and dissimilar content.

For children who know languages other than English, game descriptions may be written in the foreign language.

GAME 11   Games in History

To Enhance: Awareness of the role of recreation and physical activity in a historical context; ability to communicate verbally and in written form; ability to analyze and synthesize games and game forms.

Participants and Equipment: Children ages 8, 9, and older; retarded children ages 10, 11, and older. Variety of equipment, some of which might have to be constructed in order to provide facilities for games in history.

Description: Via library research, team of three or four children searches out what kinds of games were played at various times in history, both in this country and throughout the world. The rules of these games may be written out, and then the games presented verbally and in written form to other class members.

Modifications: Games may be confined to a specific century or to a specific country from a historical standpoint. Games may be researched, and then costumes and other apparatus which accompany the game may be made and constructed by the demonstrating children.

A research team may write about and demonstrate a series of games which represents a historical thread leading to a modern game in contemporary United States.

GAME 12   Construct and Tell

To Enhance: Written and verbal communication; sequencing and following logical progression in verbal and written communication.

Participants and Equipment: Children ages 7 and older; retarded children ages 10 and older. Construction equipment: boxes, simulated logs, sticks over which burlap or paper may be placed, etc.

Description: Group of three or more children construct a cabin, fort, teepee, or similar project, and then make up plans in written form, describing the steps in constructing their "building." A second group of children, who did not observe the previous construction in progress, using the written plans, attempt to duplicate the construction project. First group of children, or a third group, judge the accuracy of the written description, as well as the accuracy of the building carried out by the second group.

Modifications: Entire "cities," i.e., frontier villages, Indian settlements, etc., may be constructed, placed on plans, taken down, and reconstructed. Constructions may be made to coincide with social studies project. Buildings may be made to correspond to and accompany previous games in which culturally specific or historically pertinent games are described.

Initial construction team may be divided into observers-writers, workers, foremen, etc., so that a written log of the builders' efforts is formulated as construction is carried out.

GAME 13   Dance, and Say

To Enhance: Ability to engage in logical and clear written and verbal communication; appreciation of dances and dance forms from other cultures.

Participants and Equipment: Children ages 6, 7, and older. Equipment as needed for each dance.

Description: Library teams of three or four members discover dances from other cultures, countries, or historical periods. They then reduce the directions for the dance to written form, and present these descriptions either verbally or in written form to other teams of children, who attempt to replicate them in action.

Modifications: Evaluator teams may attempt to assess the accuracy of the verbal or written descriptions, or evaluate the quality of the dance efforts which emerge.

Children may contrast efforts of research groups who first translate

their dance into action before attempting written description, versus those who do not do so.

Dances researched may be made to parallel current social studies unit. Dances and dance forms may be traced historically or arranged categorically. Dance forms may be related to historical trends or to cultural characteristics from the countries from which they have emerged.

BIBLIOGRAPHY

ASHER, JAMES J. "The Total Physical Response Approach to Second Language Learning," in *The Modern Language Journal* 53, No. 1, January 1969.

CARROLL, JOHN B. "The Nature of the Reading Process," in *Reading Forum:* NINDS Monograph No. 11 (Eloise O. Calkins, Neurological Diseases and Stroke Public Health Service, National Institutes of Health, U.S. Department of Health, Education, and Welfare.

CRATTY, BRYANT J. *Active Learning.* Englewood Cliffs, N.J.: Prentice-Hall, Inc. 1971.

———. "Comparisons of Verbal-Motor Performance and Learning in Serial Memory Tasks," in *Research Quarterly* 34 (December 1963): 4.

———. *Learning and Playing: Fifty Vigorous Activities for the Atypical Child.* Freeport, N.Y.: Educational Activities, Inc. 1968.

———. "Language and Speech," in Cratty. *Human Behavior: Exploring Educational Processes.* Wolfe City, Texas: University Press, 1971.

———, and SZCZEPANIK, SISTER MARK. *Sounds, Words, and Actions.* Freeport, N.Y.: Educational Activities, Inc., 1971.

———, and SZCZEPANIK, SISTER MARK. *The Effects of a Program of Learning Games Upon Selected Academic Abilities in Retarded Children with Low Academic Potential.* Washington, D.C.: U.S. Office of Education, Bureau of Education for the Handicapped, 1971.

FROSTIG, MARIANNE, and MASLOW, PHYLLIS. *Movement Education: Theory and Practice.* Chicago: Follett Educational Corporation, 1970.

HUMPHREY, JAMES, and SULLIVAN, DOROTHY. *Teaching Slow Learners Through Active Games.* Springfield, Ill.: Charles C. Thomas, Publisher, 1970.

PIAGET, JEAN. *The Language and Thought of the Child,* translated by M. Gabain. London: Routledge & Kegan Paul, Ltd., 1926.

WEDEMEYER, AVARIL, and CEJKA, JOYCE. *Learning Games for Exceptional Children: Arithmetic and Language Development Activities.* Denver, Colo.: Love Publishing Company, 1971.

five

EVALUATION

Some scholars place evaluative processes at the top of their taxonomies of cognitive qualities. Moreover, research findings have suggested that approximately eight different evaluative abilities exist, with the possibility of five more being uncovered as the result of further investigation.

Guilford suggests that evaluation involves the following sub-operations:

1. Comparing small differences, prior to classification of combinations of letters, numbers, etc.

2. Deciding upon whether there is logical consistency in verbal statements and/or visually presented scenes.

3. Detecting imperfections or irrelevancies within various contexts.

4. Deciding which of two or more kinds of information come closer to satisfying a specific criterion.

More than one educator interested in enhancing cognitive processes has included exercises in evaluation in his workbooks and in automated programs for children and youth. Evaluative processes have also been inserted into the programs of education in which movement has been inculcated. For example:

1. An observing child may evaluate the quality of the movements made by another child, in response to such directions as "Tell me if John performs his exercise well."

2. Quantitative aspects of movement experiences may also be evaluated by participation in programs of movement education: "How high did he jump?" "How many times did he do that?" "How fast did he run?"

3. Self-evaluation may be encouraged in "movement education" programs. To measure aspiration level and related measures of self-concept, for example, a child may be asked to estimate his future performance in a task prior to its execution. He may then be permitted to perform and subsequently be asked to make estimates of predicted successes on the third and later trials.

4. A child may evaluate relative success in making correct choices or responses within an academic program in which movement plays a part. One child may, for example, jump in a grid containing the letters of the alphabet, calling them out as he proceeds, while observing children may assess the degree of success he is achieving.

Muska Mosston has perhaps paid the most attention to activities purporting to enhance evaluation within a program of movement education. In the section of his text dealing with "Reciprocal Teaching—The Use of the Partner," Mosston suggests that teaching by the "buddy system," in which one child acts as an evaluator while a second performs, has several advantages over the more traditional teacher-directed methods:

1. Most students are constantly occupied; there is little time wasted waiting in line. A student is either an active performer or an active observer.

2. The observer's self-concept is enhanced, particularly if the teacher is careful to work through the observer when seeking correct performance.

3. Each pair is given the opportunity to move along as their individual needs and abilities dictate.

4. The method gives the teacher more freedom to move around and to observe the class.

5. Immediate encouragement or correction is offered each per-

former by his partner, just after each trial, without waiting for the teacher to respond.

On the following pages a variety of games incorporating components of the evaluative processes are outlined; included are games which require the child to evaluate his own actions, his actions and capabilities in relation to others, the abilities and movement qualities of others, as well as tasks which require the child to evaluate rather abstract symbols and qualities, with movement experiences being only incidental.

GAME 1   How Far Can I ?

To Enhance: Knowledge of physical ability in selected activities; ability to modify self-estimates in the presence of concrete evidence.

Participants and Equipment: One or more children, ages 5 and older. Mat marked off in inches, for a distance of five feet.

Description: A child is asked to make an estimate of the expected distance he can execute a standing broad jump, and show, by

pointing on the mat, where he thinks he can land in an upright position. He is then asked to execute the broad jump, compare his actual jump with his previously given estimation, estimate again, and jump again.

If the children are mature enough, graphs may be drawn illustrating successive estimates and performance scores. Visual comparisons of two line graphs may then be used as a basis of discussion of goals, aspirations, life goals, how to meet one's goals, unrealistic and realistic goal setting, etc.

If children are more mature, and experienced at standing broad jumping, the less usual task of a standing *backward* broad jump may be employed.

Modifications: Other tasks can be employed in the manner described above. For a jump reach test as illustrated, first estimate, and then determine how much over a standing reach one can execute a jump reach. Again successive trials may be given, comparisons between estimates and actual performance compared and discussed.

A throw for distance activity can be employed in this manner also, as can a throw for accuracy task.

Children can discuss what happens to estimates after they have failed to reach goals, versus estimates following performance which has exceeded previous goals.

Individual differences in performance, goal setting, and just what constitutes success in motor tasks, and in life, may be discussed.

GAME 2   Which Is Different?

To Enhance: Ability to determine logical consistency and inconsistency within movement tasks; ability to evaluate similarities and differences.

Participants and Equipment: 5-10 year olds. Hoops, balls, ropes, wands, mats, gym floor or grass area.

Description: Instructor executes a group of four or five movements, e.g., jump (two feet) forward, hop (one foot) backwards, jump (two feet) sideways, three successive two-foot jumps forward, four successive two-foot jumps backwards.

Observing children must then determine which of the series of movements "does not belong" with the rest. In the group above one might say that all are forward and backward movements except one, or perhaps all are two-foot jumps except one.

Another series of movements, perhaps more or less than above, may then be executed by a child or, after planning, by one of a group of children. Observers again must determine which of several does not belong. The individual or group discovering the different movement may then plan the next series to present to the observing children.

This kind of evaluation procedure may be extended to the recognition of parts of speech, types of words, classifications and evaluations of people, places, things, buildings, etc.

Modifications: Equipment may be employed, causing more difficulty in determining differences, e.g., hoop movements may or may not be similar to each other.

Children may first plan movement series on paper prior to executing them.

More than one movement may be found to be different within a series.

Length of series may be shortened or lengthened, say, from two to six, as the children are found to be more or less capable of discovering differences.

Answers to differences may be written down prior to being announced by children.

GAME 3   Differences in Me and in My Friends

To Enhance: Awareness of individual differences in classmates; application of individual differences concept to all people in the society or sub-culture in which the children find themselves.

Participants and Equipment: Three or more children, ages 6 and older. A long rope—10 to 15 feet.

Description: Children are asked to execute standing broad jump, first one child at a time, and then several at once, using the rope in a straight line as a starting point. Differences in ability are noted and discussed.

Then children are asked to execute the same broad jumping movement, but using the rope (in a straight line) as the ending point. Again individual differences and differences in starting points are noted.

Then children are asked to employ rope as both a starting point and an ending point for the jumps of all of them, and are asked how they might lay out rope.

Possible Responses: In a circle, with children jumping across circle from circumference to circumference.

In a box, with children jumping across rope laid out in square or rectangle.

Teacher insists that above configurations are not taxing to enough children, and are too hard for others who cannot jump as far. Continues to pose question as to how rope may be used as both a takeoff and landing point so that all children are having fun (i.e., being equally taxed, relative to individual differences).

Possible Solution: Lay rope out in wedge shape, with less able children jumping across narrow portion, while more able children jump across wider portion, as shown.

Modifications: Task could be posed using rope as a high jumping "bar" and asking children to position rope to accommodate to individual differences in jumping abilities. Seek transfer from broad jumping task outlined above to high jumping task.

In both high jumping and broad jumping tasks rope may be tightened so that it is perceived as a rigid line, not as a slack arc. Then for further guidance, children may be asked to draw lines of various shapes—such as / and x—on a blackboard, seeing if they can then transfer appropriate shape from blackboard to the manner in which they position the rope for either high or broad jumping practice.

Discussion of individual differences in musical, mechanical, verbal, and other abilities might be brought out of the above concrete movement examples of individual differences.

GAME 4 Partners

To Enhance: Ability to judge performance of others, to quantitate performance, and to evaluate quality of performance in one's peers.

Participants and Equipment: At least three pairs of children, nearly the same age and abilities. Hoops, balls, ropes, mats, bats, etc.; athletic field or gymnasium floor.

Description: Following discussion of evaluation techniques, children are placed in groups of two, one designated "evaluator" and the second, "performer."

Task outlined for performers is to see if they can think of and then perform "six interesting ways to jump over something, using any of the available equipment." Make sure that the children understand that the ways must be different from each other and as "interesting as possible."

Evaluators are asked to do two things; (1) to count, to determine if six jumps are actually accomplished; and (2) to grade each jump on a three-point scale—fair, average, or good—relative to how "interesting" and "different" it is.

Make sure that children understand that they may use any equipment which is available to jump over, and that they may use it in any combination.

After evaluators observe, grade, and record, they change roles with the performers, and the process continues again under the same directions.

Care should be taken by the instructor to discuss an individual's performance only with the evaluator, not with the performer directly.

Modifications: For younger children, evaluators might be asked to assess number only, or quality only, rather than both quantity and quality of the movements engaged in.

Innumerable tasks may be proposed by the instructor or by the evaluator, including various running tasks, throwing tasks, etc. Children might also be asked to invent a game which might then be evaluated according to various criteria decided upon, which constitute the qualities needed in a game.

GAME 5 Running Differences

To Enhance: Awareness of own abilities, and comparison to others'; quantitative concepts necessary to correctly handicap running races; awareness of individual differences in many facets of human behavior, via discussion of problems and implications.

Participants and Equipment: At least 3 children and not more than 6 or 8, working together in a single group; more than one group may be employed. One stopwatch per group, measuring in tenths of a second; running area from 30 to 50 yards long, with a lightly chalked finish line.

Description: All children in group except one are asked to run a race from 30 to 50 yards long, starting at the same line. Observing child judges who finishes first, second, third, and if possible places all children in correct order of finish (more than one observing child may be needed for this).

Questions: If we continued to do these races, would the same people finish first? *Possible answers:* Yes. No, some would have more endurance than others, would depend upon how much rest time between races; some might try harder next time, etc.

Will those who always finish last continue to try hard to win? *Possible answer:* No, they will be discouraged.

How can we arrange conditions, start or finish lines, so that the race will be closer and all will have a chance to win? *Possible solutions:* Slant finish and/or starting lines so that child may start on the part of the line, either nearer or farther from the finish line, which his speed warrants, i.e. faster children have to run longer distances.

Start each child from same starting line, but at a different time, with the slowest starting first. *Additional question:* How much earlier should various people start?

Start each child from a different starting point, at varying distances from finish line, which is parallel to all starting points.

Modifications: More capable children may be clocked to the nearest tenth of a second in their first running attempt, and then their running feet in feet-per-second may be computed by dividing running speed into distance traversed, e.g.:

$$\frac{90 \text{ feet}}{3.5 \text{ sec.}} = 25.7 \text{ ft. per sec.}$$

With this information, racing distances may be computed for all participants so that all may be expected, for example, to run for exactly 4 seconds, by computing how far all might travel in that time, and placing each one that distance from the finish line. In the example cited the child should be placed 103 feet from the finish line.

GAME 6 Guess and Test Yourself

To Enhance: Awareness of own ability, concept of aspiration level, closeness of aspiration level to actual performance; concept of aspiration level in relation to mental as well as motor performance.

Participants and Equipment: Children ages 6, 7, and older; retarded children ages 10 and older. Mat laid out in 1-inch lines.

Description: Each child first indicates, from one point on the mat, a second point to which he thinks he can execute a standing *backward* broad jump.

He then must see how close he comes to his predicted mark. After each child has his turn, a discussion is held concerning how close each came to his estimated mark (i.e., aspiration level).

Children then get a second turn, preceded by an estimate, and then a third and fourth turn.

Discussion is held concerning how close performance was to estimates on first and on successive trials, why they changed estimates if they did so, and whether they felt a sense of failure or success following each performance and why.

Modifications: Estimates and performance may be graphed in the form of performance curves, which may be compared visually.

Other, unfamiliar tasks versus familiar tasks can be employed, e.g., forward broad jump, throwing a ball over one shoulder and catching it with the same hand (from a palms-upward position, with the palm backward and the arm straight and by the side), etc.

GAME 7 Arms and Legs

To Enhance: Ability to analyze self and others in movement, to analyze mechanics of movement, including throwing, running, and jumping; ability to apply analysis of movements to sports skills and self-improvement; perception of how legs and arms work in unison in sports situations.

Participants and Equipment: Children ages 5 and older; retarded children ages 7, 8, and older. Balls, jumping surface, high-jumping pit, running area.

Description: Start with questions: Do we run with our arms or our feet? Do we throw with our arms or our legs? How can I run faster, by moving my arms faster or my feet faster? How do I jump, with my arms or feet? Then have children attempt to:

1. Throw first without foot action, and then with proper step and weight-shift with foot opposite throwing arm.

2. Run slowly and then run faster, concentrating upon moving arms more rapidly; then try to run faster while keeping arm motion the same or slowing it down.

3. Try jumping up with arms at sides, with arms over head, with arms extending upward; more the arms at the same time that the legs extend and straighten at the knees, then try moving them at different times. Experiment, and evaluate which jumping method is best.

4. Try different methods of using the arms when jumping forward from two-foot takeoff. Which are best? Which *one* is best? Measure standing broad jump efforts with arms at sides, overhead, extending with and without simultaneous extension of legs at knees.

Modifications: Try to devise rules and principles for arm-leg actions in various activities. Discuss ways of improving immediate performance and long-range performance of throwing, jumping, and running behaviors. Observe best performers and weaker performers, and try to analyze why each one performs as he does.

GAME 8   Leg Power

To Enhance: Ability to perceive individual differences in leg power, and to see how one might accommodate to these types of individual differences in a competitive situation; principles of accommodating to individual differences in other skills and intellectual abilities.

Participants and Equipment: Children ages 5, 6, and older; retarded children ages 8 and older. Scale, in 1-inch increments, laid out on vertical wall surface, starting at about 4 feet above the ground and continuing to about 10 feet.

Description: Children are asked to jump up in the air. Next they may experiment with various ways of jumping upward, e.g., with and without arm movements, with arms thrown up, or sideways, or forward. Next children should be encouraged to watch each other jump, and analyze mechanics: where arms are; when they are lifted, in comparison to leg extension; and individual differences in jumping height.

Question the children as to whether all jump equally well. If not, why not? Next expose children to the scale, upon which leg power in vertical jumping may be measured. Have each stand against wall, next to scale, and extend his arms upward; now each should step back, with his side to the scale, and attempt to see how far above his standing-height-plus-reach he can jump. Measure in inches the degree of leg power each exhibits.

Modifications: Make a mathematics game out of subtracting standing-height-plus-reach from jumping-height-plus-reach. Discuss how leg power might be improved, and the question of whether leg power is dependent upon standing height.

Discuss and demonstrate how leg power and vertical jumping ability are employed in various sports, such as basketball, volleyball, and football.

GAME 9   Propelling Balls

To Enhance: Ability to analyze how to impart velocity and direction to balls, using various parts of the body.

Participants and Equipment: Children ages 7, 8, and older; retarded children ages 9 and older. Balls of various types, soccer goals, basketball hoops, backstops, etc.

Description: The object of this exercise is to determine how to do various things with a ball: How many ways can it be put into a basketball hoop from a given position on the floor? Which is the most efficient way—bouncing it in, socking it in (with one or two hands?), using the basketball backstop? What should one aim for when shooting a basket?

Soccer type ball may be used to determine how and in what manner one should kick it in order that it may go upward, travel straight, travel far, etc.

Length of leg swing as well as arm swing prior to striking a ball could be evaluated relative to the distance a ball travels.

Modifications: Study of how a ball's velocity changes when person throwing or kicking it runs toward the ball. Velocity and distances when the ball arrives at the striker or kicker with some velocity may be studied. Distances with short versus long bat may be contrasted.

GAME 10 Easy—Hard

To Enhance: Ability to critically evaluate the difficulty of games, to evaluate and organize game components, and to adjust games to individual differences in children's ages and abilities.

Participants and Equipment: Children ages 7, 8, and older; retarded children ages 10 and older. Playground equipment as needed, bases, balls, bats, volleyball nets, etc.

Description: The problem presented to the children is to invent easier modifications of playground games with which they are all familiar. These modifications, it should be explained, may make the game either more difficult (for brighter and older children) or easier (for younger children). Some examples, with possible modifications:

Kickball

Easier: Run to only one base at a time, forcing runs home; not require that a ball be caught until it has bounced once.

Harder: Require that all kicks go out of outfield, that all balls be caught on fly, that all kicks go in the air.

Volleyball

Easier: Allow one bounce before hitting the ball; permit the ball to be caught with both hands before being thrown back or to a teammate.

Harder: Ball must be hit back over the net after three hits; only overhand serves; keep hand closed on underhand hits.

Modifications: Games could be presented to either younger or older children, and their reactions observed to the modifications devised.

Children could design on paper, ways of modifying playing fields or apparatus to make game either easier or harder, e.g., lowering and making bigger the basketball rim, lowering the volleyball net, making court bigger, etc.

GAME 11 Limits

To Enhance: Awareness of the concept of an evaluation scale upon which qualities in games and other activities may be placed.

Participants and Equipment: Children ages 5 and older; retarded children ages 7, 8, and older. Variety of equipment, plus other material—boxes, brooms, wastepaper baskets, balls, hoops, ropes of all kinds.

Description: Group of two or three children invent a game using one or more pieces of equipment. Other teams of children are each given one of the following assignments: Observing the game being played, can you (1) play a similar game in either more or less space, (2) modify the game so that it requires a great deal of vigor, and again so that it requires little or no physical effort, (3) design a similar game which requires few or no rules, or many complicated rules.

Observers-inventors then demonstrate the extremes they have been able to devise. Discussion should revolve around the concept of scaling, continua, measurement, evaluation.

Modifications: The children might explore what other qualities of games might be either expanded or modified in various ways' e.g., absence or presence of thought, a few movements versus many different movements, etc.

Games devised in this manner might be applied in various ways to children who are "different"—retarded children, physically handicapped children, younger children.

BIBLIOGRAPHY

GUILFORD, J. P. *Intelligence, Creativity, and their Educational Implications*. San Diego, Calif.: Robert R. Knapp, Publisher, 1968.

MOSSTON, MUSKA. *Teaching Physical Education*. Columbus, Ohio: Charles E. Merrill Books, Inc., 1966.

six

PROBLEM SOLVING

Another important group of intellectual capacities has been termed "problem-solving abilities." This category, like the previous ones discussed, is rather amorphous and is composed of several sub-abilities, depending upon which author one consults. This classification, however, is usually considered by most to be the "highest" level of intellectual functioning, studied with reference to several rather flexible scales. Several strategies may be employed to encourage various types of problem-solving behaviors on the part of children and youth. For example, the problem posed to a youngster may require him to *synthesize,* to put together information or movements in some meaningful and original manner. On the other hand, the problem may pose a dilemma which may be solved through *analysis,* the taking apart of a more complex problem or situation, in order to extract meaning. Some complex problems require both processes of analysis and synthesis, to varying degrees. For example, within a sports situation the player must analyze his own as well as his opponent's weaknesses and strengths; at the same time, he must consider how the synthesis of his teammates' abilities and shortcomings, paired with his own, may interact when they clash against an opponent in an athletic contest.

Another scale upon which problem-solving behaviors may be studied is one that measures *convergent* versus *divergent* thinking. A problem may be structured so that there are a limited number of correct responses, or perhaps only one appropriate decision called for. On the other hand, the intent may be to prompt the learner to explore or make up a number of responses or conclusions. The first kind of task stimulates *convergent* thought, the seach for one or a few decisions; the second type of task requires what is termed *divergent* thinking, or the formulation of many appropriate solutions. It is unusual, however, to find that a problem-solving situation either calls for an unlimited number of responses or is restricted to one. Therefore, a scale may be constructed upon which may be placed a given kind of problem relative to the degree of divergent or convergent thinking called for.

Divergent Thinking			Convergent Thinking
(A) (B) (C)			(D)

Examples of tasks within programs of movement education which might fall at several points within the continuum pictured, are as follows:

(A) Extreme divergent thinking would be called for in response to the rather general directions "compose a dance routine."

(B) Less divergency would be expected if the instructions in (A) above also included the directions, "using movements of the trunk only," or "to be carried out within four minutes," or "to take place within a 10-by-10-foot square area."

(C) Moving toward the middle of the continuum, we might elicit a reasonably few "correct" choices by suggesting that a child "find six ways of moving down the mat," or by asking, "How many ways can you start the 'trip' of a ball?" If the directions "Move six *backward* ways down the mat" were given, still a more convergent response would be called for.

(D) Several extremely thoughtful problem-solving situations have been described by writers which require the selection of a single "movement solution." These lessons impose a number of conditions which, when met, permit the individual only a single response or responses within an extremely narrow band.

Piaget has suggested several further dimensions of problem-solving behavior which are appropriate to consider by those dealing in movement as a learning modality. These include:

(1) *Possibility-reality relationships.* Mature problem-solving ability, according to Piaget, involves weighing what *might be* with what *is*. The mental manipulation of operations could be handled only in concrete terms earlier in the child's life. Thus, Piaget would approve the emphasis placed upon mental trial-and-error processes seen within some movement education programs, and upon the seeking of alternative ways of acting.

(2) *Combinatorial property.* Piaget also emphasizes that mature thinking and logical operations seen in youth and children may involve the putting together of hitherto unrelated aspects of the individual's reality. Others would call this quality "creative thinking," or perhaps the ability to synthesize information as previously described. In any case, if one accepts the validity of this quality, he should aid a child to obtain "bits" of the total he may need to solve a movement problem—perhaps parts of a sequence of movements needed to traverse a vertical or horizontal distance—and then permit the child to synthesize the pieces placed before him for consideration.

(3) *Flexibility* of logical thought is emphasized in Piaget's writings as he discusses higher level thought processes. He suggests, for example, that as the youth becomes able to remove himself and his thoughts from concrete operations, he may become more flexible when seeking alternative solutions.

(4) *Reversibility.* Increased mental capacity seen in older children and youth, Piaget suggests, also permits them to perceive the manner in which logical and concrete operations may be reversed. Examples of attempts to exploit this quality in programs of movement education might include seeking ways of both getting down and getting up a ladder, or perhaps seeking to move from one point to another, moving both forward and backward. Some of the decoding and encoding that games require may tax this same quality of reversibility in the participating youngsters.

(5) *Theorizing: Discovering Principles.* Piaget and others have suggested that the ability to discover a rule and to apply the principle to more than one situation constitutes rather high level intellectual functioning. Within gymnastic lessons, basketball practice, and similar situations, students may be led toward the dis-

covery of principles applicable to a wider range of situations than the ones immediately encountered.

GAME 1   How Many Ways?

To Enhance : Divergent problem-solving behavior.

Participants and Equipment : Any number of children. Ropes, balls, hoops, wands, mats, etc.

Description: Directions can be given relative to an area on the floor, such as a mat, or with a piece of equipment, requiring that innumerable responses be designed by the children, in interacting with a piece of equipment or accomplishing some kind of movement objective, e.g., "How many ways can you move down the mat?"

Alternatives using the hoops: How many ways can you lift the hoop over your head? How many ways can you get into the hoop? How many ways can you throw the hoop?

Using the rope: How many ways can you jump over the rope? How many ways can you cross a swinging rope? A slanted rope? How many ways can you throw a rope? How many ways can you swing a rope?

Using the mat: How many ways can you cross the mat? How many ways can you get from one end to the other on the mat?

Using a line on the floor: How many ways can you walk the line? Jump over the line? Get over the line?

Modifications: Children can alternately act as performers and counters, enumerating the number of possible ways and checking so that strategies are not repeated.

The blackboard can be used to list or tally ways of accomplishing some of the movement tasks outlined above.

GAME 2   How Many, Within Limits?

To Enhance: Divergent thinking with restriction, i.e., moving from the divergent toward the convergent end of the continuum.

Participants and Equipment: Children ages 6-12. Hoops, balls, ropes, wands, mats, etc.

Description: The purpose of this type of game is to gradually model behavior relative to specified criteria, that is, to elicit not completely divergent responses, but responses which are convergent to some slight degree.

For example: Can you find some backwards ways of coming down the mat? Can you do some backwards ways on your left hand and foot? Can you do some backwards ways with right hand touching the ground? Or perhaps, Can you jump into the hoop some one-footed ways? Some turning ways? Can you start a ball moving using your left hand? Now using your left hand with the palm open, etc.

Modifications: Diagram may be made on blackboard by teacher or by observing child, illustrating how instructions gradually result in response which illustrates convergent problem-solving behaviors.

Evaluating child determines whether criteria instructions are really being incorporated into games or movements by the children.

GAME 3   One Solution

To Enhance: Convergent problem-solving behaviors, i.e., deciding within rather narrow restrictions which behavior satisfies requirements.

Participants and Equipment: Any number of children, of all ages. Variety of playground and gymnasium equipment—balls, horses, ropes, hoops, etc.

Description: Tasks may be designed so that one or more pieces of equipment are involved, or so that no equipment is involved. In the former instance, for example:

"Using this hoop can you decide how to roll it so that it returns to you along a straight line course?"

114

"Can you play a game using this rope and this ball?" The ball must be made to go over the rope, while the rope is swinging. Only two children may play the game and they may use only their left hands on the ball. Scoring should be based upon successful catches.

In the above situation it is sometimes best to gradually extend directions one at a time, until the possible response is extremely restricted, rather than giving all directions at once, particularly when working with the less mature or less able child.

Without equipment, again the possibilities are limitless. For example: "Let's see you travel down the mat, while turning, with your left foot and right hand on the mat," or perhaps, "Come to me backwards, hopping on your right foot in a straight line, ten times in a rhythmic manner."

Again the instructions may be given one at a time or all at once, depending upon the ability of the child to remember information. Instructions may be written on cards or placed on the blackboard, as well as given auditorily.

Modifications: Evaluators can determine conformity to directions. Children can devise restricted-response problem situations, using equipment or no equipment.

GAME 4   Analysis, Synthesis

To Enhance: Ability to analyze, and then to synthesize complex movement tasks.

Participants and Equipment: Children ages 5-12. Gymnasium equipment of all varieties, mats, hoops, balls, ropes, etc.

Description: Following discussion of what it means to analyze, and then to "put together" information, or synthesize, some children are exposed to a complex movement task performed by the teacher, while others are not permitted to view the action. For example, she might jump down the mat in a straight line, using first one foot and then the other, eight times overall (four with one foot and then four with the other).

Children are then asked to analyze or take apart actions. How would they describe it in one-word descriptions to another child?

Possible answers (these may be written down):
   It is an alternate action.
   It is a movement, not talking or thinking.
   It is a jumping movement.
   It is rhythmic.

It is first a left thing, and then a right.
It is movement in a straight line.
It is an eight-count movement.

Then, using the children who did not observe the action, it is attempted to synthesize the directions so that the first action demonstrated will result. They are brought back and then given one direction at a time, attempting to solve the movement problem by adhering to all conditions (alternate movement, in straight line, eight counts, etc.). Or the directions can be given all together. Solution can be presented to an individual child or to a group of children.

Modifications: Initial actions can be in conjunction with some piece of equipment.

Trials along the way, by children who are being instructed, can be accompanied by opportunities for divergent problem solving, e.g.: "How many other six-count things can you do?" "How many backwards things can you do?

GAME 5   What Is a Game?

To Enhance: Analytical behaviors, divergent problem solving.

Participants and Equipment: Any number of children, of all ages. Playground equipment and gymnasium equipment of all types, balls, ropes, hoops, etc.

Description: Teacher should pose the question, "What is a game?" After responses are elicited, continue with, "What things make up a game?" Then ask children to invent games, working in small groups, or to demonstrate commonly played games which illustrate components of games.

Teacher should attempt to encourage children to determine qualities that are always found in games, those that are found in games most of the time, and those that are found in games only part of the time. For example: Most or all games contain a beginning and an ending, movement and some thought, some joy, some rule or rules. Some games have a winner, are competitive, use equipment, have two or more people in them, require vigorous movement, have complex rules. Not all games require balls or individual pieces of equipment, require a winner or loser to emerge, etc.

This discussion may continue over a week or more in time, with frequent opportunities permitted for children to examine old games or to invent and play new games relative to the components listed, with regard to other qualities they discover, etc.

Modifications: Examine other cultural institutions—a home, a family, work, occupations, recreation, schools, libraries, etc.— deciding what, within each category, they have as common qualities.

GAME 6 The Reverse!!

To Enhance: Ability to see reverse processes within a problem-solving situation; ability to code and decode visual stimuli to movement, and vice versa; divergent thinking.

Participants and Equipment: From 2 to 30 children, ages 6 and older. Gymnasium floor, tape, geometric configurations on the floor, blackboard, mat.

Description: Using the blackboard, the children are introduced to a code, with written symbols standing for movements, e.g., 0 means jump on both feet, * means front roll on the mat. Then the children are asked to perform by moving down the mat when the teacher or a child writes the code in various ways on the blackboard; e.g.: 00, "Now do it"; or 0**0, "Now perform"; or **0*, "Now let's see who can do it."

Now moving to a geometric figure, such as a triangle taped on the floor, ask children to "jump into it." Then ask what the reverse or opposite of that would be. Expected response: "Jump out of the triangle." Then ask for demonstration of reverse of "jumping into triangle."

Using other geometric figures, children should be asked to demonstrate other movements, and then their reverse.

Now returning to the coding problem, in which 0's and *'s represented the two movements outlined above, ask children to show you the reverse of this using the length of a mat.

Possible initial responses: "Move backward down the mat" or "Move forward down the mat, but from the opposite end" (these possible solutions should be demonstrated). Or perhaps the children would want to reverse the code, i.e., *'s now mean a jump, while 0's become front rolls. All these solutions are acceptable and the children should be complimented on arriving at them.

But press the student more; ask for the reverse of the *process*. Additional cues might include: "What was done first?" One possible answer: "We moved"; correct answer: "You wrote *'s and 0's on the blackboard." "Then what happened?" "We jumped (or rolled)." "NOW what would be the reverse of this?"

Expected answer, after much struggle and contemplation: "First we move in some way, and then recorder places proper symbols on the board ! ! !" "Good, now show me. . . ."

Modifications: More than two symbols can be employed. Children can observe increasingly complex combinations of two or three movements prior to attempting to transcribe them to the blackboard. More numerous movements may be executed prior to transcribing them on the board.

GAME 7   Opposites

To Enhance: Ability to discover reverse process, ability to code and decode, flexibility, divergent thinking, short-term visual memory.

Participants and Equipment: Children ages 6 and older. Footprints, cut out of both dark and light paper, dark footprints representing left foot, while light footprints represent right foot; blackboard.

Description: Place footprints in a series on the floor but not necessarily alternated, i.e., two left footprints may be placed in front of each other, and then a right. Use about five prints at first.

After being told which color represents which foot, children are asked to see if they can move along the prints, placing their proper (left or right) feet on the proper prints.

They may be asked to see how many ways they can traverse the footprints, still keeping the correct feet on the correct prints.

Next, the children are given simple movement tasks, like those described in Game 6—such as jumping over a line forward—and then asked to show the opposite or reverse of the movement, possible responses being "jump backwards," "move under the rope," etc.

Next the children are brought back to the footprints and asked to demonstrate the opposite or reverse of that problem.

Possible initial responses: walk backwards along the footprints; start from the end and walk to the starting end, but moving forward. Perhaps the code can be reversed, making the dark footprints represent the right foot and the light prints, the left. This can proceed for a period of time, with attempts made to demonstrate more "opposite" ways of doing the problem.

= LEFT FOOT

= RIGHT FOOT

Now press, as in Game 6, for a reversal of the *process*, which is to first observe a child walking, hopping, or jumping, in innumerable combinations, and then place the proper footprints in the proper order to represent where his feet fell during his traversal.

Modifications: Various colored footprints could indicate moving on flat of foot, or on tiptoe.

Increasing the number of movements could be observed, prior to placing footprints down.

A third child could record movements on blackboard, using footprints and/or naming the movements in order.

GAME 8   Changing Codes

To Enhance: Flexibility in problem solving, coding and decoding processes, divergent thinking.

Participants and Equipment: From 2 to 30 children, ages 5, 6, and older. Gymnasium floor or outside play area, blackboard.

Description: Using four symbols, *, /, 0, and X, make up a code so that each one stands for a given movement; e.g.: * = hop on left foot; / = jump in air, both feet; 0 = one-half turn, jumping; X = kneel down.

Then to determine how well code is learned, it is written in various combinations on the blackboard: //**, X/0*, XX//, etc., and children are asked to make appropriate movements.

Code may be written with spaces between each two or three symbols. Children are asked to indicate spaces in some way, after thinking about possible ways to do so, such as leaving space on floor, delaying next combination in time, clapping hands between each combination, etc.

Now the critical part of the problem: keeping same movements and same symbols, change *pairings* of movements to code, so * might mean jump in air, etc.

Modifications: Add an increasing number of symbols to movements. Substitute words for symbols: if J means "jump," next use the word "jump" for "Jump!!" Do the same with other action verbs

GAME 9 Repeat

To Enhance: Ability to engage in flexible problem-solving behaviors; ability to remember and apply code, and to repeat code despite interfering events of a similar nature; ability to discriminate differences in movement-code relationships.

Participants and Equipment: Children ages 5 and older; retarded children ages 8 and older. Blackboard, mats, balls, hoops, ropes, etc., as needed.

Description: Children are presented with a code-to-movement problem involving three symbols on the blackboard which represent three different movements.

Then a second code is employed, using both different symbols and different movements for each symbol.

Then former code is resumed, to see if children can quickly switch to previous code-movement combinations. When and if difficulties are encountered, discussion as to why should ensue.

Modifications: More than three symbols can be employed, in either first or second code-movement problem.

Children can engage in reversing either or both problems, such as "reading" movements and then placing appropriate symbols on the board.

Children can elongate brief symbols, e.g., "R = running" equals the act of running, and "HOP" may be made to stand for the act of hopping.

GAME 10 Confusion

To Enhance: Flexible problem-solving behavior; ability to transfer from one mental-motor set to another, one sensory-motor combination to another, and back again.

Participants and Equipment: Children ages 5, 6, and older; retarded children ages 10 and older. Blackboard, variety of playground and gymnasium equipment, mats, large area for movements.

Description: Children are given a symbol-movement code problem using three or four symbols. Then the children are given the *same* symbols, but told that they now must attach different movements to them.

After this second combination of code-movement is learned, the difficulties encountered are discussed, and explanations are searched for.

Finally the children are asked to repeat the first movement-code combinations they learned, and again difficulties encountered are discussed.

Modifications: Children may learn more than three sets of symbol-movement combinations in each problem situation. In the second or first coding problem the children may also engage in the reverse process, first "reading" the movements and then transcribing the code.

Children may try to determine when within life situations—sports or other aspects of life—this type of confusion may be encountered—

A = THROW BALL

H = ROLL HOOP

T = ROLL OVER GET UP

for example, when parents say the same thing but mean something different the next time.

Children might try to react with increasing speed when confronted with the various symbols in the problem-solving situations.

GAME 11   Reversing Movements

To Enhance :   Flexibility in problem-solving behaviors, resistance to confusion caused by similar stimulus situations with opposite movement reponses called for.

Participants and Equipment :   Children ages 7, 8, and older; retarded children ages 12 and older. Blackboard, or flash cards, and variety of playground and gymnasium equipment, hoops, balls, ropes, climbing apparatus, mats, etc.

Description :   Children are introduced to a movement-code problem as follows : / = jump up in the air; 0 = roll over your left shoulder; H = execute a forward broad jump. After this is well learned and children can respond quickly as symbols are presented, the problem is changed, so that now they must execute the *opposite* movements to the *same* symbols, i.e., / = crouch down on the mat, 0 = roll over your right shoulder, H = do a backward broad jump.

Observers determine how rapidly this new code can be learned, and what causes the confusions which might exist when attempting to learn the second code.

After second code-movement problem is learned, switch can be made back to the first code-movement problem.

GAME 12   Starting and Stopping

To Enhance: Awareness of principles; application of principles to several situations; divergent thinking; awareness of physical principles governing the absorption of energy, giving impetus to objects, etc.

Participants and Equipment: Children ages 4, 5, and older. Playground equipment of all types, balls, hoops, etc.

Description: Questioning starts with "What things on the playground start and stop?" *Possible answers:* children, balls, ropes, swings. What else in life stops and starts? Lessons, school, cars, trains, etc.

Now let's experiment with how *we* start and stop. How many ways can we start ourselves? Experiment with various ways; emphasize push-off, the harder the push-off, the faster the start. Discuss acceleration, use of arms when moving legs faster, etc.

Now how do we stop? Observe each other. How can we stop most quickly? Consider effect of lowering hips; observe stopping without and with the lowering of center of gravity.

How many ways can we start a ball? Demonstrate with feet, arms, etc. How do we start a ball on a long fast trip? Observe each other; Is arch of arm or leg increased, and/or what happens when a ball is thrown harder toward limb hitting it? Can we start a ball with parts of our body other than a hand or foot?

How can we stop a ball? Demonstrate "stopping power" of curtain or cement or wooden wall, when ball is thrown against it. Apply principle of a "giving curtain" to the human arms and hands when catching a ball. Ask for demonstrations of how else a ball may be stopped.

Modification: What can we do to a ball in order to produce different pathways, spins, velocities, arcs, etc.?

Discuss principles which regulate movement, stopping, and starting of balls and of people, as well as of other thing. Discuss mechanical devices which permit acceleration and deceleration of vehicles, including rockets.

GAME 13 Adding Equipment

To Enhance: Ability to analyze game components, to synthesize components into total game situation, to be flexible when developing games.

Participants and Equipment: Children ages 7 and older; retarded children ages 10 to 12 and older. Variety of playground equipment, "junk" equipment (pans, wastebaskets, brooms, etc.), plus balls, hoops, ropes, mats.

Description: Children are given one piece of equipment or they select a single piece of equipment, and then they are asked to invent a game in which it is employed. Then a second piece of equipment is selected, or added by the teacher, and the request made that the game be changed to include the second item—the original form of the game should remain, however.

A third piece of equipment is added, and the game expanded further; a fourth is added, and so on.

Modifications: More than one performer might start with the same game using one piece of equipment, and then two or more groups might work independently when pieces are added. Evaluators might then assess the separate directions the games have taken in the hands of the different performers working independently.

After pieces of equipment have been added one at a time, they might be taken away in the same manner, and further game modifications sought.

GAME 14   Hoops and Targets

To Enhance: Ability to engage in divergent problem solving and convergent problem solving; flexibility in problem-solving behavior.

Participants and Equipment: Any number of children, ages 5, 6, and older. Balls, hoops.

Description :   Object of the game is to devise a game in which the ball may be thrown or bounced through one or more hoops. First the following directions are given to the children: "Make up a target-throwing game."

Now can you devise a target-throwing game involving throwing the ball through all three hoops as they are held in a vertical position? Now can you work out a target-throwing game in which the hoops are held overhead, and the ball either bounced or thrown through all three hoops?

Now can you work out a target-throwing game in which the ball is both bounced through a hoop placed horizontally, and also must travel through one or two hoops placed in a vertical position?

Now can you invent a game in which the ball must be thrown through three vertical hoops that are held together so that the ball will barely fit through?

Modifications :   Can you now invent a game in which four hoops are employed as targets? A game in which the hoops are placed in at least three planes, as the ball is employed in a target-throwing task? etc.

GAME 15   Reverse Obstacle Course

To Enhance: Ability to reverse problem-solving situation, flexibility in perceiving new directions for efforts and movement modifications in a similar situation.

Participants and Equipment: Children ages 5, 6, and older; retarded children ages 10 and older. Equipment permitting an obstacle course to be constructed—fences, barrels, boxes, targets, etc.

Description: One child (or a team of children) is permitted to construct an obstacle course using the equipment available, and then is asked to negotiate each obstacle in any way he may choose.

Observing children are then asked to reverse the obstacle course as the teacher points out that there are several ways to "reverse" the problem.

The concept of "reverse" or "do it backwards" may have to be worked out in a simpler context for younger children; e.g.: "Jump in the circle." "Now what is the reverse of this?" "Jump out again."

The variety of ways in which this problem may be reversed should become apparent to most children, and they should be asked to act out their solutions: going down the obstacles in the opposite direction, reversing the order of the obstacles, moving through the course backwards, or perhaps reversing the movements (or making them in an opposite manner) which were required to negotiate each obstacle.

Modifications: Children may work with only a two-dimensional obstacle course, in which configurations are painted or taped on the ground. Vertical courses might be worked out using a climbing apparatus.

Children should be presented with mental problems in which reverse solutions, and means-ends relationships, are sought.

GAME 16   Select the Rules

To Enhance: Ability to classify and to synthesize rules into a game "whole."

Participants and Equipment: Children ages 6 and older. Various pieces of equipment—balls, hoops, ropes, etc.; at least 12 cards, on which individual rules are printed, such as "score one for jumping over", "three throws limit," and similar instructions.

Description: Children are asked to select two to three rules out of a box containing the cards. They are then asked to invent a game which fits the rules they have selected.

Children acting as judges are then asked to determine if the games invented indeed do fit the rules selected.

Modifications: Children may be asked to first select a single rule, then make up a game which it fits; then select a second rule, and change the game so that both rules fit it; then select a third, modify the game again, etc.

Children may be asked to pick five rules, and then invent a game which fits any three of them.

One group of children may be asked to select three rules and devise a game which two of them fit, then observing children may be asked to determine which two of the three rules were acted upon by the group initiating the game.

GAME 17   Analyze and Change

To Enhance: Ability to analyze complex behavior; ability to reform components into a new whole, i.e., synthesize; ability to engage in diverse problem-solving behavior.

Participants and Equipment: Children ages 6-12. Game equipment appropriate for familiar childhood games—playground balls, backstops, balls and bats, ropes, etc.

Description: Children are asked to observe a familiar childhood game, such as dodge ball, kick ball, or baseball.

They are then asked to analyze it into its component parts; e.g., volleyball means hit a ball, get it over a net, serve the ball, prevent it from hitting the ground, hit it underhand, hit it overhand, etc.; kick ball means kick a ball, run from base to base, catch a ball hit in the air or rolling on the ground, etc.

Next the children are asked to take the component parts of the game and rearrange or change them so that a new game is developed. This may take the general form of the old game, and should contain all or most of the parts of the usual game, but should evidence different characteristics.

Modifications: One element of the familiar game may be omitted, and a new element inserted. Two elements may be omitted and one or two inserted, and so on until the game changes entirely.

Game may be modified for either younger or older children, by being made easier or more difficult.

GAME 18   Combine and Change

To Enhance: Ability to synthesize parts into wholes, ability to analyze wholes into component parts, ability to engage in divergent thinking.

Participants and Equipment: Children ages 7, 8, and older; retarded children ages 10 to 12 and older. Game equipment plus junk equipment of a variety of kinds—balls, cans, tires, ropes, hoops, mats, etc.

Description: Children are first asked to analyze parts of a complex game they have made up, or the parts of a familiar game.

Next they are asked to combine parts from two or more games into a different "whole" game.

Evaluators might assess the extent to which a truly different game has been developed, as well as the extent to which they retained the parts of previously observed or played games.

Modifications: Children may select parts from each of four games, either familiar or newly made up, to make up a different game. A circle dodgeball game might borrow an element from kickball, with the ball being kicked at children in the middle of the circle to get them "out." Volleyball and sockball might be mixed by requiring children in a volleyball court to catch and sock the ball back to opponents.

GAME 19 The New With the Old

To Enhance: Ability to engage in library research; ability to analyze and to synthesize, to create something new out of familiar, but previously unrelated parts.

Participants and Equipment: Children ages 6-12. Game equipment of various kinds, balls, bats, music; library references.

137

Description: Children are asked to go to library, individually or as a group, and to find games which have been played during past history, either in this country or in foreign countries.

They are then asked to demonstrate the game they have found in their library search.

Finally they are asked to combine the old game they have researched with a more modern and familiar game they have played recently.

Evaluators judge the quality of the researched game and the creativity exhibited as the new game emerges from old and new parts.

Modifications: Children might discover more than one old game and combine it with parts of other researched games.

Evaluators and performers reverse roles after games are first demonstrated and combined.

Modifications which are appropriate for younger as well as older children might be devised, of both the new games and the historical games.

GAME 20   United Nations

To Enhance: Ability to engage in library research, ability to synthesize and to analyze, ability to exhibit flexible problem-solving behaviors.

Participants and Equipment: Children ages 8 to 10, and older. Variety of familiar as well as unfamiliar playground and gymnasium equipment.

Description: Children, via library research or through foreign students in their school, discover and learn to play games employed in other lands.

These games are then analyzed into component parts, and compared with games played in the United States which are familiar to them.

The foreign games may then be combined into entirely new games, or combined and modified using games with which the children are already familiar.

Modifications: Music needed for some foreign games may be employed as background for familiar or newly created games.

Games of history may be combined with foreign games.

Foreign games may be analyzed in a context provided by other national characteristics of the country from which the game has emerged and developed.

seven

THOUGHTFUL RULES

IN A CHILDHOOD GAME

A most fruitful way to study the interraction between mental and bodily activity is to observe the manner in which children invent, conduct, and play a game, without direct adult intervention.

During recent years, a very popular form of handball has been played by elementary school children in many parts of Los Angeles. The game uses a large rubber playground ball, about 8 inches in diameter, which is hit against a large backboard, approximately 12 feet wide and 12 feet high. The ball may be hit by one or both hands, and unlike the faster-moving adult handball game, not only is the ball allowed to strike the ground after rebounding from the board, but it is also usually hit so that it strikes the ground a second time before striking the backboard again. Points are scored if the ball bounces twice before being hit by a player, or if it bounces twice after being hit and prior to restriking the backboard.

This game is particularly amenable to study because of several factors. A large number of children at white middle-class schools play the game every day (from 70 to 80 percent, according to estimates of children I have interviewed) ; the rules are reasonably consistent from school to school but vary interestingly between schools, between sexes, and between grade levels. These differences will be discussed shortly.

Furthermore, not only is the game popular, but it is truly the children's own creation. Rules for the game are not found in curriculum guides supplied by the boards of education. Most of the teachers in the schools I visited had heard apparently important expressions called out by the children as they played the game, but had only a vague idea or no idea of the nature of the rules.

From expedience and by trial and error, the children have over the years developed ingenious modifications of the rules which have several effects upon the game and its participants.

1. An unlimited number of children may participate, either as spectators, waiting in line to play, or as periodic players.

2. Competition is maximized, as individual differences in skill between players are reduced to a minimum.

3. The rules permit a great deal of intellectual, verbal, and lawyer-like behavior to be incorporated into the motor skill components of the game. Arguments during the game are frequent.

Rules and Terms

The number of rules that the children have developed for this game is almost endless. The list below includes only some of them. Also the terms and expressions used may vary from school to school.

1. *Babies:* When a ball is hit so that the rebound occurs close to the backboard, preventing or making a return difficult.

2. *Cross-country:* When a ball is hit so that it takes a lateral pathway across the court, from left to right to left, making a return difficult.

3. *Backliners:* When a ball is hit hard so that on the rebound it crosses the endline, taking a high bounce, and making a return

difficult or impossible. Called *outliners* when the same thing occurs over one of the sidelines.

4. *American:* When a ball is hit so that it does not take an intermediate bounce before striking the backboard. The term is sometimes applied to a ball that is hit after it rebounds from the backboard without an intermediate bounce.

5. *Pops:* When the ball (usually with a backspin), traveling at about a 45 degree angle, hits both backboard and ground at the same time, and pops up close to the board.

6. *Slices:* When a ball is hit so that it assumes excessive spin, making the subsequent return difficult or unpredictable.

7. *Waterfalls:* When a ball is hit with a high arch, strikes the backboard and slides down vertically, and bounces straight up near the board, making a return difficult or impossible.

8. *Overboards:* When the hit or served ball goes over the backboard; point is scored against the hitter or server.

9. *Blocks:* When one player "interferes" or gets in the way of another attempting to return a ball.

10. *Pink elephants:* When a child reaches the front of the waiting line, he may be asked to run across between the winning player and the board, while the ball is thrown at him. If hit by the ball, he forfeits his turn to play and must go to the end of the waiting line.

11. *Sets:* The number of turns that each player will be allowed to play the ball (i.e., catch or stop, then hold and rehit the ball) during any particular game. This number is agreed upon before the game starts, and is indicated by the first player up, who "taps" his foot on the court and says "two sets" or "three sets" or the number of sets agreed upon.

The manner of playing the ball during a set is also usually decided in advance. After catching the ball, the player may serve it in the regular way, i.e., by holding the ball with one hand and hitting it with the other, or in the manner called "sticking it" whereby the ball is thrown up into the air and struck with both hands clasped together.

12. *Selfs:* If so agreed, a player may serve the ball to himself and return it to the backboard before it is hit by the opponent.

13. *Everyday catches:* If "tapped" (i.e., agreed upon), each player may execute as many sets (see 11 above) as he wishes during a game.

The Game in Action

Armed with a knowledge of terms, let us see how the game is played, modified, argued over, and otherwise manipulated within various contexts and within various age levels and sex groupings.

Most of the time the game is played on a one-to-one basis, one player "taps" first, and plays a one-point game with the second player. The waiting players line up, and enter the game one by one, after one of the first two players in the game has been eliminated. Most of the time the new player does not have to run the gauntlet (see *pink elephants,* above).

The waiting players are seldom silent and usually, in addition to providing general encouragement, vocally remind the players of the agreed-upon rules as situations occur during the playing period.

Rules governing the game are agreed upon in two ways. A certain number—specific to the grade, sex, or court—are already known by all in advance. A number are flexible, and must be either "tapped" as they are spoken, such as *everyday catches,* or are argued about during the course of the game.

If left to their own devices, the children will usually stay with the one-one-one game, work up, and eliminate players after a single point. Playground directors might set up more elaborate after-school tournaments, but this practice is met with indifference or even hostility on the part of the children.

Modifications for Age and Sex

The most interesting aspect of this game is the manner in which it is modified to meet the skill levels and needs of children of various ages. For example, third and fourth graders generally play with more rules, eliminating as "fair" balls that are hit or rebound in ways difficult to return. Thus, in their games, *pops, waterfalls, backliners, slices,* and *babies* are considered "unfair" and do not count; if they occur, the game must be restarted with a new serve.

Gradually, as a child grows older and gains more proficiency, the rules that make the game easier to play are eliminated. Indeed, they are later disdained by the fifth- and sixth-grade children. Moreover, most of the children we spoke to were aware of general differences in the skill level and strength of boys and girls in the later elementary school years, and again the games were made easier for the girls by the insertion of the rules outlined above. Thus, for example, it is often possible to find a fifth-grade girls' game containing several more of the "make-easy" rules than are present in the boys' game in a similar grade.

On the other hand, strict division by sexes is not always carried out. That is, the more capable sixth-grade girls will seek out a game in which fifth-grade boys are participating, in order to find more challenging competition. Most of the time the games do contain both boys and girls in the waiting line.

Implications for the Development of Meaningful Play Experiences

It is apparent that due to the fact that the children have devised the handball game over a period of time, or due to the ingenuity of children in a given situation, the game serves a number of needs. It is active, requires force when hitting the ball, employs strategy, and requires exact interpretation and employment of a number of rules.

Moreover, it has become easily modifiable, serving at many levels of difficulty, depending upon how many of the "make-easy" rules one chooses to employ. Thus a simple form may be engaged in by children aged 7 and 8, while a more advanced, but similar form may be played by children of 10 to 12.

Most important, it has not been taught in a formal way by teachers or physical educators, nor is it contained in curriculum guides to which either might have referred. Rather, in the schools where we conducted our surveys, it was common to find that, if they bothered at all, the first- and second-grade teachers did indeed teach games to their charges—but games which they were extremely *unlikely* to engage in during their remaining elementary school years. Rather, they would adopt games played by their peers, such as handball; children teach themselves games which are valued by their peers, not those contained in curriculum guides which may have been prepared years earlier by those out of contact with the needs and desires of contemporary children.

Children in the early primary grades soon develop marked needs to do what the older children are doing—in this case they can hardly wait to play handball, or at least some simplified version, as soon as they are able. They do not repeat, and barely tolerate the games introduced to them by their teachers, most of whom are not familiar with the real games being played by older children and the often complex systems of rules which govern these games.

Additionally, it is common to see children whose motor skills may be less well developed approach the game of handball from an entirely different viewpoint. These less adept children often function more as "lawyers" than as athletes. They constantly argue about the rules which are in force, and the interpretation of those which seemingly are acceptable to the players. Indeed these "arguers" seem to revel in the intellectual and verbal exchanges they create. Thus the game seems to fulfill the intellectual needs of some, while meeting the action needs of others.

It would thus seem that the manner in which this child-invented game has emerged, and appears, affords several principles for the development and expansion of movement experiences for children.

1. Rather than developing games with rigid rules, it might be attempted to devise what might be termed "game forms," which guide children toward types of movement experiences while affording flexibility. For example, the concept of relay races might be introduced, as I recently saw in an elementary school. The vigor and variety of relays, especially those devised by black children, was incredible!

2. A variety of games or athletic forms might be introduced, and preceding each a discussion of rule modifications could take place, modifications which would permit children of varying skill levels to participate either together or separately.

3. Games could be devised by the children which permit, indeed encourage, argumentative behaviors. Perhaps a game which would allow frequent changes of rules, either as it is taking place or between rest periods, would be interesting. In this way the needs of the "lawyer-athletes" on the playground, as well as those of the "athlete-athletes," might be met. If basic provisions were made in games for rule change and discussion, there might be less animosity seen between children whose needs are primarily to participate versus those who enjoy verbal interplay during the course of the contest.

4. Most important, individuals interested in devising meaningful physical education curricula for younger children *should not* start with preconceived plans, but rather should observe what the older peers of the children desire when attempting to satisfy movement needs. Teachers in the primary grades might thus seek, during the primary years, to prepare their children for the games which these children are going to take up anyway, as a result of

their needs to do what the older children are doing, as well as due to their exposure to the games of their revered elders.

In conclusion, it might be suggested that curriculum planners and sensitive teachers can in operational ways hasten the development of meaningful and physically developing game forms; such development would bypass the period of evolution which was apparently necessary to arrive at the interesting game of handball with its variety of helpful and useful modifications. Moreover, in the development of game forms, the principles of modifiability for individual skill differences, flexibility of rules, and accommodation to needs for argumentation might be met in situations which require a greater variety of physical response than does the game outlined in this chapter.

BIBLIOGRAPHY

DULLES, F. R. *America Learns to Play*. New York: Appleton-Century-Crofts, 1965.

HOLLIMAN, J. *American Sport, 1785–1835*. Durham, N.C.: The Sieman Press, 1931.

HUIZINGA, J. *Homo Ludens: A Study of the Play Element in Culture.* London: Routledge & Kegan Paul, Ltd., 1949.

LOY, JOHN W., JR. and KENYON, GERALD S. *Sport, Culture, and Society*. London: The Macmillan Company, 1969.

LUSCHEN, G. "Die Funktion des Sports in der modernen Gesellschaft" (The Function of Sport in Modern Sociey), in *Die Leibeserziehung*, Germany, 1963, V. 12.

MCINTOSH, P. C. *Sport in Society*. London: C. A. Watts Company, 1963.

NATAN, A. *Sport and Society*. London: Bowes and Bowes, 1958.

eight

OVERVIEW

AND APPLICATIONS

A brief look will now be taken at the manner in which thoughtful games may be employed, as well as at the type of child who might benefit from exposure to them. As with all such suggestions for special deviations from traditional school programs, their success depends upon the teacher's accepting them wholeheartedly, having a thorough understanding of the objectives of each game, and possessing the creativity necessary to provide conditions and instructions which introduce novelty into the learning situation. A teacher endowed with neither creative instincts nor commitment to at least occasionally try something new (and thereby admit that in the past she was not 100 percent correct in the offerings she devised) stands little chance for success within the context outlined here, or in most types of learning environments.

How Used?

The various games described in Chapters 2–6 have not been subjected to detailed experimental analysis, but have been derived from a review of the literature dealing with intellectual abilities, together with a survey of the types of physical activities which might be employed to stimulate these same abilities. For these activities to be effective, however, the teacher should follow several guidelines.

It is very important that teachers focus not merely upon the motor behavior of the participating youngsters, but rather upon the type of intellectual quality they aim to enhance. Furthermore, instructors should rely on passive as well as active means for eliciting use of the intellectual abilities outlined. Thus, for example, in a lesson focusing upon the concept of individual differences, a discussion should ensue before the children are led into working within a movement milieu. The children should be encouraged to *talk* about, to give illustrations of individual differences, so that they may express themselves in ways other than through tasks requiring obvious, overt action.

To cite another example, the thrust of the lesson might be to discover what it means to engage in divergent thought. A discussion might be encouraged through which to discover various life situations in which divergent thought might be appropriate, for example, when composing a song, devising creative advertising campaigns to sell products, or perhaps recommending ways to preserve the ecological balance of a nearby forest. After the discussion, in which most of the children may have begun to grasp the concept of divergent thinking, the children may be led into one or more movement examples of what it means to devise numerous solutions within a problem-solving situation. Through this means, some of the children may be better able to conceptualize about the idea of divergent thinking through active means. At the same time, this type of "acting out" of various conceptual operations permits the observing teacher to determine the extent to which the concept has truly been grasped by the participating children.

Following this type of active involvement, further discussion may take place, exploring other facets of problem-solving behavior, or perhaps trying to extend the type of problem-solving behavior into one or more of several possible directions. For example, one might at this time explore how various games within the culture stimulate the intellectual abilities to varying degrees. Or the children may be asked to devise further movement games which illustrate the ability under consideration. In graphic form, the manner in which discussion blends into active games, which in turn might lead to further discussion and movement experimentation, is illustrated by the following diagram.

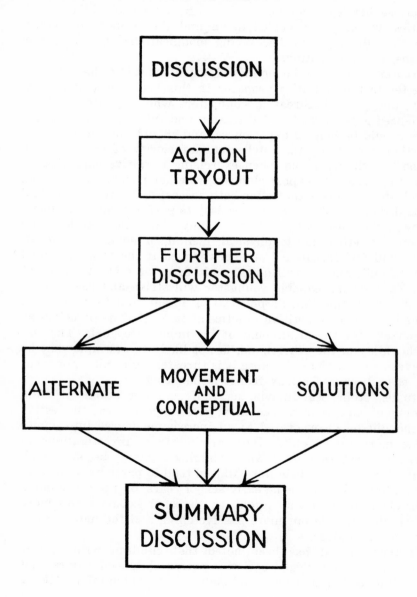

For Whom?

Consider also the various types of children for whom "thoughtful games" might be appropriate. For example, it is obvious that the younger normal child might find them happy and helpful ways to exercise his legs and mind. Even the preschool child, if the activities are carefully scaled down and the proper vocabulary employed, will have fun discovering modifications of games, new solutions, new applications.

Greater care must be employed when exposing the retarded youngster to the activities proposed in this book. One must start simply, and pose no threat to youngsters who may already have experienced a great deal of frustration and failure. Games of this nature should be helpful experiences, and should not become ways of further confirming the intellectual inferiority of children who may be less than capable when exercising cognitive capacities.

It is necessary to expose children, whether normal or retarded, to a "cluster" of tasks that offer both success and stress. If a child is provided only tasks that he finds easy to perform, he is not likely to grow, either physically or intellectually. The child with learning problems—whether due to physical, mental, or emotional impediments—will feel threatened or overwhelmed if the task presented is too difficult, and he will quickly withdraw or make no attempt at all. The normal, capable youngster will strive and reach when presented with the difficult physical or intellectual task, but will become bored with repetitive practice at tasks that he perceives as unimportant for the attainment of his immediate goals. The less capable child, on the other hand, is not likely to attempt what he perceives as too difficult, because it is threatening to him, nor what is too easy, because he may feel it is insulting.

Studies from Scandinavia, as well as observations of child development experts in this country, give support to the suggestion that thought be incorporated to an increasing degree into games for the more gifted child. Data arising from investigations in Norway suggest that only when childhood games become intellectually taxing do the brighter children tend to participate in them during late childhood. In the early school years, on the other hand, rather clear-cut divisions might be detected between the more intellectually capable but more passive child, and the more active, less cerebral children.

Furthermore, it has been noted that children within more "advanced" and privileged societies prefer childhood games that require intellectual endeavor, and spurn those which offer little or no intellectual challenge. Children within these more sophisticated cultures become well aware, at an early age, of the qualities which are likely to serve them well in adulthood. Even the less perceptive realize that it is brains, not brawn, that will be responsible for their later successes in life. These children, as is traditional with children in all cultures, consciously or unconsciously select games that call into play attributes which are later to become important to them.

Especially in modern societies do children require movement for proper maintenance of their bodies. Various illnesses associated with degeneration of bodily processes are occuring to an increasingly higher degree among the young, including heart disease, stomach ulcers, and muscular-circulatory disorders.

Thus, it would seem sensible, particularly within modern societies whose environments and values tend to stifle physical exercise, to incorporate activity and thought into the same lesson. It is believed that the games outlined, therefore, should be carefully considered by those working with both gifted and normal youngsters.

Further Uses

There may be further uses for the types of activities outlined. For example, employing them singularly or in groups, one might construct a reasonably culture-free intelligence test, as was attempted by Stanley Porteus several decades ago using pencil-maze tests.[1]

Active games may be employed as a kind of reward or activity break in school schedules, which many times are oppressive for children with high activity needs. Games of the type outlined might also be employed within regular physical education classes, alternating with or at times completely replacing the more traditional ones dictated by the culture.

Summary

Games that require various kinds of intellectual behaviors have always been found in the culture. If one were to analyze, for example, a kickball or dodgeball game, it would be possible to

---

[1] Stanley D. Porteus, *The Maze Test and Clinical Psychology* (Palo Alto, Calif.: Pacific Books, 1959).

isolate various processes involving memorization, evaluation, categorization, and problem solving which are important in their execution. At the same time, the games this book more specifically "zeros in" upon are concerned with various facets of intelligence which have been identified by various scholars during the past twenty years.

These games must be placed correctly within a total educational context; their effectiveness depends upon the degree to which the teacher administering them possesses insight into the needs of the children involved. The ability to adjust to the intellectual and maturational levels of various kinds of children is a further requirement which an instructor entering the world of movement and thought must acquire.

Games of the type outlined may be correctly employed to aid the slow or retarded child to think and to act in more concrete and effective ways. Furthermore, these, activities may stimulate the average or the gifted child to engage with verve in physical activities he has previously disdained as dull or unchallenging.

BIBLIOGRAPHY

BLOOM, BENJAMIN, ed. *Taxonomy of Educational Objectives, Handbook I: Cognitive Domain.* New York: David McKay Co., Inc., 1956.

CRATTY, BRYANT J. "Cognitive Operations," in Cratty. *Human Behavior and Learning: Understanding Educational Processes.* Wolfe City, Texas: University Press, 1972.

———. *Physical Expressions of Intelligence.* Englewood Cliffs, N.J.: Prentice-Hall, Inc., 1972.

ELLIS, HENRY. *The Transfer of Learning.* New York: The Macmillan Company, 1965.

FROSTIG, MARIANNE, and MASLOW, PHYLLIS. *Movement Education: Theory and Practice.* Chicago: Follett Educational Corporation, 1970.

GAGNÉ, R. W. "The Analysis of Instructional Objectives for the Design of Instruction," in Robert Glaser, ed. *Teaching Machines and Programmed Learning, II: Data and Directions.* Department of Audiovisual Instruction, National Education Association, Washington D.C., 1965.

HUNT, J. M. *Intelligence and Experience.* New York: The Ronald Press Company, 1961.

MOSSTON, MUSKA. *Teaching Physical Education.* Columbus, Ohio: Charles E. Merrill Books, Inc., 1966.

PIAGET, JEAN. *The Origins of Intelligence in Children,* translated by M. Cook. New York: International University Press, 1952.

STAATS, ARTHUR W., and STAATS, CAROLYN K. *Complex Human Behavior.* New York: Holt, Rinehart & Winston, Inc., 1963.

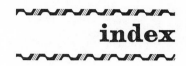

index

157